PREGNANCY AND INFANTS: MEDICAL, PSYCHOLOGICAL
AND SOCIAL ISSUES

A DARWINIAN GUIDE TO PARENTING

HAVING A BABY

PREGNANCY AND INFANTS: MEDICAL, PSYCHOLOGICAL AND SOCIAL ISSUES

Additional books in this series can be found on Nova's website under the Series tab.

Additional e-books in this series can be found on Nova's website under the e-book tab.

PREGNANCY AND INFANTS: MEDICAL, PSYCHOLOGICAL AND SOCIAL ISSUES

A DARWINIAN GUIDE TO PARENTING

HAVING A BABY

LINCOLN G. CRATON

AND

SHARON RAMOS-GOYETTE

publishers

New York

LIBRARY OF CONGRESS CATALOGING-IN-PUBLICATION DATA

ISBN: 978-1-63482-066-0
Library of Congress Control Number: 2015930588

Published by Nova Science Publishers, Inc. † New York

To our families

CONTENTS

PART I. EVOLUTIONARY SELF-HELP: THE APPROACH IN THIS BOOK

Chapter 1

INTRODUCTION

Becoming a parent is like starting a long-distance swim. Once you decide to take the plunge, you are in it for the long haul. Along the way, you'll find that there are times when you struggle to keep your head above water. There are certain difficult questions that all new parents and parents-to-be must answer for themselves:

- When is the "best" time to have a baby?
- Why isn't getting pregnant easier?
- Why do pregnant women find healthy food nauseating, but only in the first trimester?
- What's the "normal" amount of weight to gain during pregnancy?
- Why do so many women experience heartbreaking miscarriages?
- If childbirth is so natural, why does it hurt so much?

These may seem like unrelated questions, each with their own separate answers. In fact, most pregnancy, birth, and baby books and magazines do treat them as separate. But they're not.

Many parents are looking for a way to make sense of *it all*, to tie it all together. We want more than just tips and techniques to help us get through the many daily challenges of new parenthood. We want a way of looking at our new family situation. We want the big picture of the parenting swim.

Is there such a thing? Is there a single perspective that can help us understand why becoming a parent is the way it is? Is there a single way of looking at parenthood that we can bring to bear on virtually every practical parenting question we will ever have? There is, but you won't find it in most parenting books or blogs.

The parenting gurus of today have plenty of useful tips. But in the long-distance swim of parenting, the most useful and inspiring perspective comes from an unexpected source: Charles Darwin. Looking at parenthood from an evolutionary point of view is like climbing out of the water and looking down from an island mountaintop. Once you see your life from this aerial perspective, you'll find that you have a powerful tool to help you answer any question you have about becoming a parent.

THE SINGLE GREATEST IDEA EVER

Applying evolutionary thinking to the practical everyday concerns we have about having a baby is simple. You just need to understand one thing: evolution by natural selection. Many people are already familiar with Darwin's great idea. But if you're not, don't panic. Here are three reasons why it's worth spending ten minutes or so learning about it:

- It's *easy* to understand. So easy, in fact, that when Darwin first explained it to the world a hundred and fifty years ago, a zoologist named Thomas Henry Huxley exclaimed, "How stupid not to have thought of that!"
- It is a really, really *good* idea. Tufts University professor Daniel Dennet has even gone so far as to suggest that it is "the single greatest idea ever," because it can answer so many of our questions about life.
- It is a profoundly *useful* idea for anyone having a baby. Read on, and you can become a wiser, happier, and, yes, a better parent.

Any idea that is so simple, so powerful, and so useful to parents is worth finding out about, don't you think? Whether you have already taken the parenting plunge or are preparing to do so, it's a good time to become a Darwinian dad or mom.

The next chapter briefly explains evolution by natural selection and how it helps parents. The rest of the book applies evolutionary thinking to the most common and pressing questions we ask when we have a baby.

Chapter 2

HOW AN EVOLUTIONARY APPROACH HELPS PARENTS

In the previous chapter we compared becoming a parent to starting a long-distance swim. We suggested that evolutionary theory gives us an aerial perspective on the swim of parenthood. It allows parents to get out of the water and look down at our life as if from an island mountaintop.

When we get worked up about a parenting issue, we find that a trip up this mountain helps us put things in perspective. Not only do we end up understanding the problem better, but we also *feel* better about it. We become calmer, better able to make good decisions that benefit our families and ourselves.

The deep understanding and the serenity that evolutionary thinking provides can be a tremendous help as we conceive, carry, give birth to and nurture our babies. So come with us to the top of the mountain and let's spend a minute looking at your life from the evolutionary viewpoint.

PROBLEMS THAT EVERY PARENT WILL FACE

As you climb, the first thing you'll notice is that from here, you can see all of the moms, dads, sons, and daughters on the planet. Just take a look at that mass of humanity swimming down there! Over seven billion and counting.

Notice what happens as we get closer to the summit. The higher we get, the more similar everyone looks. When we're in the water, the differences between people are what stand out. There are good evolutionary reasons why people normally pay close attention to these individual differences…but for now let's notice, from this distance, the similarities. As we climb higher, details fade from view. You'll notice that all humans start looking, well…pretty much the same. That's because in many ways, we are. You just need to get some altitude to see it.

What do you know? All the people down there have two arms, two legs, and a head. Never really thought about that before! After you watch for a while, you'll start to notice that we share more than just physical characteristics. There are also many ways of behaving, thinking, and feeling that all people have in common, as we will see throughout this book. Since every human being on the planet has them, psychologists call these physical, behavioral, and mental characteristics "universals."

Ah, here we are. The summit. You can't really make out the individual characteristics of people from up here, and so what really stand out are all the universals. Take, for instance, just one of the many challenges that all parents must face: a baby's crying. Normally, we might focus on the fact that one baby cries more than another—especially if that baby is ours. But up here we notice the interesting fact that *all babies cry*. Normally, we might notice that one parent seems more tolerant of her crying infant than another parent does. Up here, we notice the interesting fact that *all adults find an infant's crying hard to take*.

Congratulations! You've just taken the first step in an evolutionary approach to parenting. You've started paying less attention to individual differences and more attention to universals. Individual differences will be important, too, but not until later. First we have to figure out why certain traits are universal. Why do all babies cry? Why do all adults find crying hard to take?

WHY BABIES CRY AND WHY PARENTING IS THE WAY IT IS

"The answers are obvious," you might say. "Babies cry because they are wet, hungry, or need physical contact. Adults find crying hard to take because it is loud and unpleasant." And of course, you would be right. But that just leads us to ask "why" again. Hunger, for instance, is just the immediate cause of a baby's crying. Psychologists refer to this as the *proximate* cause. But we can still wonder why on earth a baby should be built to emit an unpleasant sound when it requires nutrition! To understand this, we have to go beyond the *proximate* cause—the immediate, obvious cause—of the baby's behavior to what psychologists call the *ultimate* cause of the baby's behavior: why did it evolve?

To find the ultimate cause of a human universal like crying in infants we must turn to the "single greatest idea ever": the theory of evolution by natural selection. Although scientists and scholars still debate the details of the story, everyone accepts the simple but far-reaching insight that Darwin provided: each of us is a product of a process called evolution by natural selection.

What does this amount to? Well, many folks know what evolution is already. That's the old idea that living things change over many generations. Natural selection is what Darwin figured out; it's what makes evolution happen. It involves two things: variation and selection.

Variation just means that different individual living things vary in some of the characteristics they are born with. Selection happens when a characteristic helps an individual survive and reproduce. This characteristic shows up in the individual's young. A trait that tends to get an individual dead, on the other hand, won't get passed down to offspring: there won't be any! When natural selection works this way for many generations, you get universals.

Each of us has the physical, behavioral, and mental characteristics that helped our ancestors survive and reproduce.

And that's about all you need to know about natural selection to read this book.

HOW TO BUILD A BABY

Now, how does anyone figure out the how a universal behavior like crying, for instance, helped babies survive? By doing "reverse engineering." It sounds fancy, but the basic idea is simple. Linc knows about reverse engineering because his brother-in-law, Francois, once interned at a company that designed computer systems. Except that they didn't do much designing, exactly. They did reverse engineering.

Basically, reverse engineering involves taking someone else's design and figuring out how it works so you can reproduce it and sell it. It's a pretty common approach. According to Francois, figuring out someone else's design—in the absence of any documentation—is extremely difficult. You start by opening it up, examining one part at a time and asking, "What's this *for*?"

A growing number of scholars from a range of disciplines are using reverse engineering to understand human behavior. Let's say you want to understand why some universal behavior in children evolved. Like the computer hardware that Francois tried to figure out, children do not come with any documentation. But don't worry. No one is disassembling any kids! Instead we ask, "What's this behavior *for?*" In other words, how does this behavior help children survive?

In the case of infant crying, we can begin to speculate that natural selection built crying behavior into babies because it helped keep a caregiver close, increasing their chances of survival. For this to work, it would have to be a sound that would grab the caretaker's attention. Congratulations again! You have taken the second step in using an evolutionary approach to parenting. You used reverse engineering to figure out why kids cry.

Reverse engineering works as a research strategy because, like computers, humans actually have been designed. You, your children, and all the people you will ever know were designed by natural selection.

THE CAMPING TRIP FROM HELL

It's not always easy to figure out why a particular universal trait evolved. One big problem is that for almost all of human existence, people lived as hunter-gatherers. It was a mere 10,000 years ago that agriculture was invented, and industry emerged in just the past few hundred years. These modern developments are much too recent to have influenced evolution much. What this means is that natural selection has designed us for an ancient, foraging way of life. So when we ask, "What's this behavior *for?*" we aren't asking how it promotes survival in the modern world. We're asking how it promoted survival in the ancient world of our hunter-gatherer ancestors. This means we need to know something about that ancient world. Do we?

Scientists disagree about the details. But if you take away modern technology, industry, and agriculture you start to get a pretty clear picture of ancient hunter-gatherer life. Basically, it was the camping trip from hell: never-ending and without modern conveniences of any kind. If you have ever gone car camping, you will be able to picture the kind of horror we are talking about.

Let us remind you about car camping. Picture this: First, you pack the car with many arguably necessary items like tents and stoves and lanterns and, of course, a lot of food. If it is perishable food it's in a cooler and you will have to eat it that day. You drive to a campground, find a designated campsite and turn in to the parking spot provided. You next unload your camping equipment and pitch your tent somewhere between 10 and 30 feet from your car. There is a lot to do and it is not nearly as convenient as being home, but once you are set up there is time to hike around and, later, to sit around the campfire. Do you have an image in your mind?

Now take away the home where you packed up. Take away the car and the roads you traveled on to get to the campground. Take away the packaged food, the cooler, the campground, and the tent, stove and lantern. Do you have the image? Now think about this: Ancestral life was the image you now have, day after day, without cease.

Oh, we almost forgot. Take away hot showers, too.

It was no utopia. An ancient hunter-gatherer's life prospects included frequent near starvation, sickness, and big animals that viewed you as food. The main tasks were hunting animals and gathering plants for food, avoiding becoming the food of predators, mating, and...*caring for your kids*.

Many psychologists now believe that we evolved a host of specialized mental tools that helped us do these jobs. As a result, we are a bit like Inspector Gadget, a detective from an old cartoon show. This guy has a collection of special devices—hammers, helicopter blades, and so on—that pop out of his head whenever he needs them. The difference is that Gadget's tools are actual gadgets and gizmos, and they are designed to help him catch bad guys. Ours is a *mental* toolkit, and it is designed to help us and our little ones survive an ancient, foraging way of life.

ULTIMATE ANSWERS FOR PARENTS

At this point, you may wonder how knowing why some trait evolved— what psychologists call the ultimate cause of the trait—can help you make parenting decisions. For us parents, the *ultimate* answers we seek are not about evolution at all! They're about what to do with our kids.

Knowing the evolutionary story behind human universals can help us understand our parenting experience. As a result, *it can help us make all sorts of parenting decisions.*

Take childbirth. On Wednesday, May 18 at 2:51 a.m., as Linc looked into his beautiful newborn daughter's face and she gazed back at him in that quiet, alert way that newborns do, he mostly felt relieved that both she and his wife were all right, safe. It had been a long, hard labor ending in a c-section. Had wife Paule not had the c-section, their daughter and possibly Paule herself might have been in mortal danger. "Why was this so hard?" Linc wondered in the happy drowsy hours before he finally went to sleep.

Although this labor was particularly grueling, it turns out that birth is universally hard for humans. Only evolutionary theory can give us a compelling explanation for why this is so. And once you understand why, you are in a much better position to plan the type of birth experience that is right for you.

The example of childbirth is instructive because it points out that parenting from an evolutionary perspective is not the same thing as a "back-to-nature" or "natural family living" approach. While natural childbirth techniques are very helpful, that doesn't mean we want to outright reject potentially life-saving medical technology. Applying evolutionary thinking to parenting means understanding human nature, the way people and their babies are designed, and using that understanding to make parenting decisions that work for us. That is not the same thing as trying to become an ancient hunter-gatherer!

Nevertheless, it is useful to take notice when modern parenting practices and the ancient evolved design of children are out of whack with each other. There are many ways in which our modern lives no longer match the lives that natural selection designed us for. For starters, ancient hunter-gather women

- hit puberty later than contemporary girls do
- had no form of birth control
- gained only about fifteen pounds during pregnancy
- carried their babies throughout much of the day and slept next to them at night
- nursed their children through toddlerhood
- had a stable network of relatives that helped with child care and work
- had intervals of three or four years between the birth of their children, and
- remained lean and muscular throughout their lives.

Once you've identified mismatches such as these the job becomes deciding what to do about them. The answers are not always so clear.

Sometimes we might want to modify the prevailing modern cultural practice so that it approximates more closely what the ancient hunter-gatherers did. But this is not always possible or even desirable.

As you'll soon see, there is often a set of trade-offs that parents have to consider when choosing between modern parenting options and methods that more closely resemble the ancient practices that humans are built for. Only after we understand the tradeoffs involved can we decide whether doing things differently will be worth the effort.

A QUICK CAVEAT AND THEN ON TO THE SHOW

It is easy to make up evolutionary explanations for things. Researchers refer to highly conjectural, unsupported evolutionary explanations as "just so stories," after Rudyard Kipling's fanciful children's tales. It takes some training and familiarity with the scientific literature to recognize the difference between a well-founded evolutionary story and a wildly speculative one.

It's likely that you don't have the time right now to immerse yourself in the field to sort out the quality work from the pseudo-science! In this book, we've done the hard work of separating the wheat from the chaff. Throughout, we try to note how well-supported the various evolutionary scenarios are. But we didn't want to clutter up the book with a lot of citations to scientific papers. So if you want to look into the science on which the ideas in this book are based—and they are based on solid science—you can find reading lists and other material on the Darwin's Child website (*darwinschild.com*). As for this book, a glance at the table of contents provides a quick overview of the topics to be covered. Feel free to jump around.

PART II.
BEFORE YOU DIVE IN:
SOME THINGS TO CONSIDER

- What is your menstrual IQ (see Chapter 3)?
- When is a good time to start a family (see Chapters 4 and 5)?

Chapter 3

THE MENSTRUATION SITUATION

What do minstrels have to do with it?
-Ten-year-old son, in response to older sister's conversation with friend

Although they tend to know more about the subject than men (and 10-year-old boys), even women are sometimes bewildered by their menstrual cycles. And no wonder! Women from earlier generations, in particular, often received very little information about their cycles. Untold numbers of young women in the 1950s and earlier were literally frightened by their first periods. No one told them this would happen! Sometimes they just had to figure things out for themselves, like the woman we know who was so uninformed that for months she tied the little string to her underwear for fear that her tampon would never come out again.

The menstrual cycle is a universal. All women cycle. What is this process, exactly? Why does it work the way it does? Why does it affect us—both women and yes, men—the way it does? Even if you know the basics, the complete scientific answers to these questions are surprising and complex. For moms- and dads-to-be, understanding some of the technical details of female reproductive biology will prove helpful. And learning about the evolutionary origins of this mysterious biological system just might amaze you and help put it all in a grand perspective. In particular, this topic highlights our species' highly social nature and what that means about the way family life evolved.

DR. RAMOS-GOYETTE'S MAGICAL MENSTRUAL TOUR

We begin with a down and dirty description of the physical changes that occur during every woman's monthly cycle. Second, we summarize how the modern birth control pill or—more accurately—pills, work by impacting this cycle. Third, we ponder the causes of the changes that occur during the menstrual cycle. Recall from the last chapter that psychologists like to distinguish between the *proximate* or immediate cause of a universal trait and the *ultimate* cause of it, that is, the reason it evolved. In the case of an infant's crying, the proximate cause might be hunger or pain, but the ultimate cause is that it promoted the infant's survival.

Ok, what about the menstrual cycle? Let's describe it and explore the proximate causes both inside and outside a woman's body that affect it. Then, let's explore the ultimate or evolutionary reasons for this distinctive aspect of women's lives.

ANATOMY (AND PHYSIOLOGY, AND ENDOCRINOLOGY) OF A PERIOD

It may be surprising to learn that "the" menstrual cycle actually encompasses two distinct cycles, the ovarian cycle and the uterine cycle. The ovarian cycle is responsible for the release of the hormones you may already know like estrogen and progesterone. The uterus changes in response to these hormones, and this is the uterine cycle. It is true, too, that the same hormones that are causing changes in the uterus also cause changes in behavior. Mood and cognition also change over the menstrual cycle, as we will see.

The Ovarian Cycle

At birth, baby girls have thousands of eggs. Over their lifetime, these eggs die through a process termed "atresia." Although it sounds bad, this is a normal process. Many of our cells will undergo programmed cell death if they don't receive the signals they need to continue to grow. Around the time of puberty, the pool of eggs begins to mature. Only one egg progresses to the point of ovulation each month, but the hormones that are secreted during each monthly cycle help prepare a group of the remaining eggs for their turns. The ovarian cycle can be divided into four components.

Follicular Phase

The egg is surrounded by a group of cells. This layer of cells, called the follicle, completely encompasses the egg. These cells enlarge and secrete estrogens at high levels. The estrogens act on the egg to mature it. The follicle also secretes something called "antral fluid" into the interior of the follicle, surrounding the egg. As the time of ovulation draws near, the antral fluid expands. This first stage of the ovarian cycle in which the cells of the follicle are multiplying and the space between the egg and the follicle fills with fluid, is called the FOLLICULAR PHASE. By the end of this phase, it looks like the egg is inside an over-filled water balloon, just waiting to burst. This is called the Graafian Follicle.

Ovulation

The ovary, where all of this is happening, is actually not attached to the fallopian tubes. The fallopian tubes contain a finger-like structure at their end, called "fimbrae." In response to a hormone called oxytocin, the fimbrae sort of pinches the swollen ovary. These pinches on the nearly bursting Graffian follicle actually cause the follicle to rupture–not unlike a water balloon! The antral fluid and the egg rush out. This is OVULATION. Some women can feel the effects of oxytocin and experience anything from a tiny pinch to a sharp pain when they ovulate. Some women who experience pain and bleeding during ovulation may have a condition called Mittleschmertz.

Fertilization

Now that the matured egg has been released, fertilization in the fallopian tube is possible. If fertilization does occur, then the fertilized egg will undergo several rounds of cell replication and make its way down to the uterus, where it will implant. Implantation occurs about 7-10 days after ovulation. This can be accompanied by bleeding, which can be confused with a short, early period.

Luteal Phase

Now, back in the ovary, the follicle that had been producing estrogens and fluid and maturing the egg, is still back there. It is still producing hormones! Now, it is producing high levels of progestins as well. At this stage, the follicle looks different than it did while the egg was present. It eventually develops a yellowish appearance and is called the corpus luteum, or yellow body.

Because this stage is characterized by the corpus luteum, it is called the LUTEAL PHASE.

In the absence of signals from a fertilized egg, the corpus luteum will live about 14 days. Toward the end of that time, the cells of the corpus luteum begin undergoing programmed cell death. Fewer and fewer cells are available to make hormones, so we have less and less hormone. The cells continue to die and consequently, hormone levels become very low. The cells begin dying shortly after ovulation. Thus hormone levels begin a precipitous decline about a week before the period. This is why Premenstrual Syndrome (PMS) occurs *before* the period. PMS is a response to a slow loss of hormones.

The Uterine Cycle

Let's look now at the uterus and its lining. The interior of the uterus is called the endometrium. ("Endo" means "within.") During the uterine cycle, the endometrium matures and secretes hormones. This process of preparing the endometrium for implantation is called decidualization (which means "ripening" and comes from the same root word used to describe fruit trees). Decidualization is an interesting aspect of human reproductive physiology: a woman's endometrium begins preparing for implantation before ovulation has occurred, early in her cycle—whether fertilization occurs or not. In many other species, decidualization occurs only if fertilization occurs first.

Proliferative Phase

Estrogens produced by the ovaries during the follicular phase of the ovarian cycle cause the endometrium to enlarge. Because the cells in the endometrium are undergoing a high level of proliferation, this component of the uterine cycle is termed the PROLIFERATIVE PHASE.

Secretory Phase

After ovulation, the corpus luteum secretes high levels of progestins. Under the direct influence of progestins, the cells of the endometrium shift their function. Instead of continuing to proliferate, they begin to specialize and secrete a variety of molecules. This is termed the SECRETORY PHASE. These secretions optimize implantation and appear to be at their highest levels about seven days after ovulation, which marks the beginning of the window for implantation.

Menses — The Period

Meanwhile, the endometrium has grown a new system of blood vessels to supply the rapidly dividing and differentiating cells of the endometrium. If fertilization does not occur, the same decrease in hormone levels that underlies PMS causes the blood vessels in the endometrium to regress. Soon, the recently enlarged endometrium can no longer be supported by the diminishing blood supply available. The endometrium begins to fall away from the uterus, sometimes bringing its corkscrew-shaped blood vessels with it. The tearing away of the endometrium causes bleeding or menses—what we call the "period."

CONTRACEPTION – HOW TO DEFEAT MOTHER NATURE

One of the most popular forms of contraception is "the pill." Just as we simply say, "the menstrual cycle" and actually mean something really complicated, "the pill" is really lots of different kinds of pills. If you polled a group of women who were actively avoiding pregnancy by taking "the pill," chances are that very few women would be taking exactly the same prescription. Even so, the mechanism of action for many "pills" is similar. Just prior to ovulation, there is a huge surge of LH (the hormone measured in ovulation predictor kits), accompanied by a huge surge of estrogen. Ovulation occurs only when there is that continuous rising of estrogen over a period of time. "The pill" works by keeping estrogen levels exactly the same each day, until you have the placebo week. It prevents ovulation from occurring by preventing any increase in estrogen levels.

When the pill first came on the market, the estrogen levels in it were very high. Too high, in fact. Estrogens affect other aspects of physiology besides the initiation of ovulation. For example, estrogens have profound effects on our cardiovascular system. The pills that came out caused life-threatening blood clots. So, estrogen levels were diminished in "the pill" and now, many pills also include small amounts of progestins. The difference in the many "pills" out there is, among other things, the levels of estrogens and progestins they contain.

Because the estrogen levels in pills are now lower than they used to be, timing is important. If you take the pill at 7:00 am one day and then 8:00 pm the next, then, the following day, you are back to 7:00 am, the body may interpret that as a slowly rising increase in estrogen, which may lead to ovulation, depending on how consistently the pill is taken in the following days.

Some "pills" do not include placebos and in this case, since the estrogens that nourish the growth of the endometrium remain at a steady level and do not decrease, there will be no menses. However, the endometrium is still building up. Therefore, most pills that work this way require a wash-out period about four times a year. In other words, women on this kind of pill have four periods a year instead of 12.

We do not know of any long-term study on the use of "the pill." Nowadays, a young girl who is just beginning puberty may immediately be put on the pill. If she starts taking the pill at age 12, then by the time she is say, 25 and ready to have children, she will have been on the pill for 13 years. What we do know about short-term use of the pill is that it increases the risk of breast cancer and decreases the risk of ovarian cancer, which is less common, but also more life-threatening. What we don't know is what happens when one takes the pill for a decade, as is becoming more common. We would not advocate teen pregnancy, for many reasons. But we also would warn against exposing girls to something that has not been studied extensively. There are readily available barrier methods of contraception that also prevent the transmission of STDs which, at this point in time, seem safer and equally effective.

A fairly recent development has been the advent of the "morning after" pill. This one works a bit differently, by blocking the progestin receptor. Progestins are essential for the development of the embryo. In fact, the name "progestin" is derived from the more cumbersome "pro-gestational hormone." Blocking progestins right after potential fertilization will prevent further development and implantation of the embryo.

PROXIMATE CAUSES—EVENTS OUTSIDE THE BODY CAUSE UNPREDICTABILITY

The entire chain of events that describes the menstrual cycle can be thought of as a series of internal proximate (immediate) causes that occur, one influencing the other. One internal proximate cause leads to the next, in a cascade of events in a woman's body that repeats itself monthly.

In women and some other primates, events outside the body also influence the menstrual cycle. A major and often overlooked characteristic of the human menstrual cycle is its variability. The reproductive cycles of other mammals are relatively fixed and predictable. If human reproductive cycles were predictable, a woman would always have a 28 day cycle every single cycle, no matter what. A normally cycling healthy woman trying to get pregnant would know the very first day of a missed period, definitively, that she was pregnant. Such a thing seems so foreign, so in contrast to our normal experiences, that it's actually hard to even digest what it would mean. Among other things, the market for over-the-counter pregnancy predictor kits would be non-existent!

The luteal phase of the ovarian cycle is highly predictable; the 14 day life-span of the corpus luteum is fairly stable. That's why women are advised to count backward 14 days from the first day of the period to determine the day of ovulation.

It's the follicular phase of the ovarian cycle where variability in timing comes into play. The developing follicle responds to signals coming from the brain, for instance in the form of gonadotropin releasing hormone (GnRH). GnRH elicits the release of other hormones (LH and FSH) to which the follicular cells respond. GnRH (and LH and FSH) levels can change in response to many factors, such as stress and pheromones from other women (leading to synchronization of cycles among women living together).

ULTIMATE CAUSES: A TALE OF TWO REPRODUCTIVE CYCLES, ESTROUS AND MENSTRUAL

Look up the definition of menstrual cycle, and you may find something like "physiological changes that take place that allow for the maturation of the egg and preparation of the uterus for implantation." We agree. But that definition doesn't take us very far. It does not tell us much beyond what most women already understand from their own experience of the reproductive cycle. Once you start pondering *why women evolved to cycle in the way that they do*, things get a little more interesting.

A useful and fascinating way to elaborate on this basic definition—and to begin to see things from an evolutionary perspective—is by contrasting the human menstrual cycle with the reproductive cycles of other species. We can compare creatures with respect to three factors: the presence or absence of menses (bleeding), the timing of sexual receptivity, and whether ovulation is easily detectable by other members of the species.

Menses

The estrous cycle of most mammalian females does not include menses or bleeding. Women, of course, experience copious menses when they have their period.

Sexual Receptivity

Females of most mammalian species have a kind of reproductive cycle that biologists call "estrous." What most women find surprising, almost shocking, about estrous cycles in other animals is that sexual receptivity—the actual ability to mate—is confined to the very narrow window of ovulation. In this way, ovulation is tied to sexual receptivity, theoretically optimizing the likelihood of fertilization. This is obviously not the case with women, who have menstrual cycles and have the ability—if not necessarily the desire or energy—to mate all the time, any time.

Concealed/Advertised Ovulation

Finally, females in estrous typically advertise ovulation using visual cues (e.g., a red rump), vocalization, or other means. In contrast, women often don't seem to know when they are ovulating and importantly other members of the group do not know. However, lots of new data suggest that everything from changes in a woman's behavior to changes in the responses of others occur during ovulation, so ovulation is not as concealed as was once thought.

This combination of copious menses, extended sexual receptivity, and concealed ovulation that characterizes the menstrual cycle of human females is fairly unique among mammals.

The traditional notion of the estrous cycle is that it is the very opposite of the menstrual cycle, with a narrow window of sexual receptivity, no menses, and advertised ovulation. It turns out, however, that these three factors combine in many different ways across mammalian species.

For instance,

- Some quantity of menses can be found in several primate species; even bats have some bleeding (LC—Thanks Dr. Ramos-Goyette, you just gave me a great idea for my next Halloween costume!)
- In some primate species—particularly those living in multi-male, multi-female groups—menses occurs but sexual receptivity is confined to ovulation and females advertise ovulation with both visual cues and vocalizations

- In other menstruating primate species such as chimpanzees and baboons we find that advertised ovulation is coupled with a sexually receptive period that extends beyond ovulation, but is not continuous.

What are we to make of this cross-species complexity? It is only in a few species, like humans, that we begin to see all of the components of the menstrual cycle emerging together. This suggests—at least to evolutionary biologists—that the suite of characteristics as modern women experience them did not evolve all at once or suddenly appear in the first human.

Why did menses evolve? Because the large endometrium that is built up during decidualization cannot be reabsorbed into the body, as it can in other species with smaller uteruses or less decidualization.

Why did extended sexual receptivity and concealed ovulation evolve? We believe that the best explanation has to do with the fact that in ancient hunter-gatherer life, one person could not successfully raise a baby alone. Human babies have big brains and are helpless at birth and for a long time afterward. Promoting the baby's survival (providing food, etc.) and protecting the baby from harm (from predators or others in the group or a terrible fall) requires constant vigilance and effort. One way to maximize survival and minimize threats is to surround the baby with adults who are—or think they could be—related to that baby. Extended receptivity, concealed ovulation, and the frustrating unpredictability of the menstrual cycle all probably evolved because in ancient society, one adult was not enough to raise a human baby. Check out chapter 6 to find out some of the eyebrow-raising details.

Chapter 4

YOUR AGE

Now, here, you see, it takes all the running you can do, to keep in the same place.
                    -The Red Queen, in Lewis Carroll's Through the Looking-Glass

One way to become a happy parent with happy children is to start having kids when the time is right. When is that? Is there an ideal time to have your first baby?

PREHISTORIC FAMILY PLANNING

A girl gradually learns how to support herself and by age 15 is quite self-sufficient. She lives among her relatives, mostly from her mother's side of the family. She has her first period at 16 or 17. Not long after that she gets married. Although her brothers leave the group to find wives and then settle among the families of their wives, she remains within her "natal" or birth home. The couple never uses any birth control, and the girl gets pregnant at age 19. Pregnancy and nursing force her to slow down a bit, but her husband and other relatives help put food on the table, and other women in her group nurse her baby occasionally. At first she takes the baby with her everywhere, but as the child gets older other people close to the woman help out. She nurses the child for four years. When the child is finally weaned, the girl—now a young woman—quickly becomes pregnant again. This pattern repeats itself several times throughout the woman's fertile years. Altogether, she has about 100 periods throughout her life and she gives birth seven or eight times, though some of these are stillbirths.

"Whose life is this?" you may ask. It's probably not anyone you know. For one thing, women living in Western cultures experience about four times as many periods over a lifetime as this woman: 400, not 100! Rather, this is a rough description of a hunter-gatherer woman's life long before the invention of agriculture 10,000 years ago. Based largely on observations of modern-day hunter-gatherer groups by Beverly Strassman and other dedicated anthropologists, evolutionary biologists figure that this is pretty much the way it was for virtually all of human existence. This way of living evolved from components of biology that already existed in our primate ancestors. It is, in an important sense, the life that women were "designed" by natural selection to have. But this does not mean that it is an ideal, desirable, or even feasible life for anyone living in the technological world of the 21st century.

Let's call this woman and her husband, who lived so long ago, Hannah and Harold Hunter-gatherer. Hannah had three things going for her that most modern day Moms do not:

- *Youth*—she started having kids as soon as she was reproductively mature, at a time when she was approaching the peak of her fertility.
- *People*—she had her first child knowing that she had a committed husband and a strong, stable network of people to help provide food, protection, and child care.
- *Resources*—she had her first child only after she could support herself reasonably well, which for her meant knowing survival skills like how to use tools to gather and prepare food.

Youth, people, and resources: surprisingly, despite the many benefits of living in a modern society, parents today are often lacking in one or more of these positive factors when they have their first child. Why should this be? We will explore the answers to this question here and in the next chapter. In this chapter, we focus on the advantage of youth.

Part of the answer is that with the invention of modern birth control and reproductive technology, we have disconnected sex from pregnancy. The basic plot of Hannah and Harold's family life was all laid out for them. Before the development of modern birth control, couples did not really have the option to choose when to start a family or how many children they might have. Once they got together, Hannah and Harold didn't have to make a whole lot of decisions. As we will see, things are a lot more complicated now. Like dazed supermarket shoppers faced with too many brands of laundry detergent, we are both blessed and burdened by the range of reproductive choices we now have. Having these options changes the ancient pattern of family living. If we make a point of being well-informed and conscious of this dramatic change, then we can make the best possible decisions based on our individual situations. To do so, we should begin by understanding how the family life that we were designed for fits—or doesn't fit—with the world we live in. In other words, we need to know about Hannah and Harold, and compare their family lives with the various ways that family life unfolds in our more complicated modern world.

Consider the following true story. As is the case with all the real-life anecdotes in this book, the names have been changed to protect us from being assaulted by family, friends and acquaintances (for simplicity, married couples have hypothetically chosen to share the same last name):

Deborah and Donald Delayer

A woman has a series of relationships after graduating from college, but remains uninterested in marriage despite having a number of suitors. Meanwhile, she gets her work life together. By her late 30's she is making a steady income when she finds the right guy. In his 40's, he is a reliable wage earner. He's also crazy about her, and the feeling is mutual. The couple fall in love and get married. However, they have trouble conceiving. She has a heartbreaking miscarriage at age 40 (when he is 50), but is able to get pregnant again two years later. As I write this, her first child is due in about three months. She will become a mom at age 42; dad will be 52.

How does the Delayer's situation compare to that of Hannah and Harold, the Hunter-gatherers? Like Hannah, Deb has a committed marriage partner as well as friends and family (*people*). The Delayers both have stable jobs with steady incomes and live in a privileged modern society in which they do not have to forage for food each day to stay alive (*resources*). However, in order to get these people and resource advantages (and, admittedly, to enjoy single life for a while), Deborah has put off trying to conceive until the very end of her natural reproductive years (*youth*). In fact, she has managed to put off starting her *family* life until a time when some anthropologists believe that ancient hunter-gatherer women would be nearing the end of their *entire* lives. Is this a good idea?

We know a lot of people like Deb and Don, and you probably do too. Thanks to modern birth control, they were able to put off parenting until they felt ready. According to the conclusion of a 2013 Gallup Poll in the United

States, "Some medical experts say the best age for a woman to have a child is in her late teens or early 20s, because that is when she has the best odds of conceiving a healthy child. However, that doesn't square with modern Western sensibilities about pursuing higher education and career goals, finding the perfect partner, or simply relishing the experience of young adulthood. Given this tension between biology and societal norms, the decision about when to start having children is a highly personal one. Hence, Americans give a wide range of answers when asked what the ideal age is for women—and, separately, men—to have their first child."

Despite the considerable variability in response, this poll found that the average *perceived* ideal age to have a first child was 25 for women and 27 for men. Although current and reliable estimates for the *actual* average age of first-time moms and dads are not readily available (especially for dads), it is clear that both men and women have been delaying parenthood more and more in recent years.

Unfortunately, this is not great news. As it turns out, the Delayer's experience highlights some advantages of having children earlier rather than later.

One problem is that nature has designed Deborah—all women, in fact—to reproduce between the ages of 19 and 40, like Hannah the Hunter-gatherer. Waiting as long as the Delayers have is risky in a few ways: it makes it more difficult to conceive, it increases the chances of miscarriage, and it increases the likelihood of having a sick child. We'll address each of these risks in turn.

HOW TO BE A FERTILE MYRTLE

Although Deb and Don were eventually able to conceive, they might not have been so lucky. It was quite difficult for Deb to get pregnant. Like all human females, she was born with a supply of thousands of unripened eggs. Like all women, Deborah's fertility declined gradually from her 20's on. It really started to nose-dive at around age 40. By age 51—currently the average age of menopause—she will be completely sterile, with her egg supply nearly depleted.

So, a possible cause of the Delayers' heartache was the fact that Deb's reproductive system had been designed by natural selection to begin shutting down at age 40. The way to be a fertile Myrtle, it turns out, is to conceive earlier than most modern women do. Why should this be?

MENOPAUSE — AN ADAPTATION?

Menopause is a curious fact of life. The eggs of some other animals remain viable for much longer than 50 years. Why didn't natural selection design women to keep reproducing all their lives? Wouldn't that allow them to bear more children overall? Isn't that what natural selection is all about?

Until recently, some biologists had thought that the female reproductive system shuts down at 40 because ancient hunter-gatherers rarely lived past that age. Since our lifespan has consistently increased only very recently in our evolutionary history, they reasoned that natural selection has not had time to push menopause back to an older age. This makes some sense, but it doesn't explain why our other biological systems—our heart and lungs, for instance—don't shut down after age 40. It also wouldn't explain why men, who theoretically would have died roughly around the same age as hunter-gatherer women, don't have reproductive systems that completely shut down by 51.

The other possibility is that hunter-gatherer women often survived beyond age 40, and that those who did experienced menopause just as modern women do. Menopause might have evolved because as a woman aged she could do more to increase the number of people containing copies of her genes by helping her existing children survive to adulthood, and by helping her grandchildren and her other relatives, than by producing yet another child. This idea, called "the grandmother hypothesis," proposes that menopause was adaptive for our ancient ancestors. It makes a lot of sense, when you consider that by helping existing family members rather than producing more of them, an aging hunter-gatherer woman also eliminated the risk of dying during childbirth or from the struggle to feed yet another hungry child.

The grandmother hypothesis also fits well with what we know about ancient patterns of dispersal in women. As we'll discuss in more detail in chapter 5, when Hannah grew up she stayed to live with her relatives; her brothers, on the other hand, went off to stay with the families of their wives rather than their own family. This is generally true of mammals: if one sex disperses from the natal group and the other sex stays, it is usually the male who leaves and the female who stays. There is good evolutionary logic in this. Maternal grandmothers and aunts can *always* be sure that their grandbabies, nieces, and nephews are biologically related to them. Alas, this is not true for paternal grandmothers and aunts.

We don't currently know with certainty whether the grandmother hypothesis is correct, although there is good evidence across different cultures from different historical periods that maternal grandmothers tend to improve children's survival, and do so more consistently than either paternal grandmothers or even fathers.

MISCARRIAGE – A PAINFUL ADAPTATION

The grim truth is that miscarriage is a common event at any age, although we usually aren't even aware that it's happened. Most miscarriages occur before the twelfth week of pregnancy, which is why it is traditional to share the news of the pregnancy only after the third month. Many miscarriages occur before a woman would even miss her period. In fact, an astonishing 78 percent of all fertilized eggs either fail to implant or are spontaneously aborted before a woman knows she is pregnant. Unfortunately, Deborah was farther along with her pregnancy and was all too aware of the fact that she had miscarried.

Perhaps, like us, you will be somewhat reassured to hear that most miscarriages occur because there is a chromosomal or genetic abnormality in the fetus. These problems are called "embryonic lethal," because whatever is missing or messed up is critical for life. Natural selection has designed mothers so that their bodies can sometimes detect these serious abnormalities. This ability evolved because it prevented ancient hunter-gatherer mothers from investing time and energy in a baby that was likely to die young: given our ancestral environment, it would have been best for both the mother and baby to start over and spend that time investing in a future child who would be more likely to survive and reproduce. It may be some consolation to the Delayers to know that the baby-to-be they lost probably had a serious impairment and if so, would have suffered if it had survived longer.

Why didn't Deborah miscarry earlier in her pregnancy? One possibility is that the problematic gene or genes in her baby-to-be did not "come online" right away. Not all of the genes a baby-to-be needs for life are turned on upon fertilization. During the early development of the embryo, certain genes are turned on—those involved in replicating cells, for example. Equally critical, though, are genes that remain off until the "right" time—like those involved in maturing lungs for taking in oxygen. (Think what would happen if the developing fetus began to try to breathe in air while immersed in amniotic fluid.) So it is possible—and of course, heart-breaking—for an embryo to begin to develop and then stop. The genetic problem that caused Deb and Don's miscarriage may have been with genes that turn on late, genes that were perhaps involved in making the heart, liver, or brain.

In addition to alterations in genes, there are chromosomal abnormalities to consider. These are probably more familiar to most parents-to-be. As a woman's eggs get older her chromosomes are less likely to separate properly. The bottom line is that as a woman gets older, the chance of chromosomal abnormalities shoots up and, consequently, so does the frequency of miscarriages. For the Delayers, their loss was all the more sad because it was not at all clear that they would get another chance at parenthood, at least by natural means. Happily, Deb was able to get pregnant again. The next risk the Delayers face concerns the health of their child.

Chromosomal abnormalities aren't always lethal. That is good news, but it's not ideal. Children born with chromosomal abnormalities are often sick and tend to have shorter life-spans. The risk of giving birth to a baby with chromosomal defects increases dramatically as a woman reaches Deb's age. The overall rate of chromosomal abnormalities rises sharply from 1 in every 190 at age 35 to 1 in every 10 pregnancies at age 48. To take a more specific example, the risk of having a baby with Down Syndrome increases from about 1 in 1,900 births for a 20-year-old mother, 1 in 280 for a 35-year-old, and 1 in 65 for a 42-year-old, to 1 in 15 for a mother at age 48.

SPERM OF THE MOMENT: RISKS ASSOCIATED WITH OLDER DADS

Until recently, even experts would have assumed that Deb's age was the cause of her miscarriage. We now know that it is quite possible that the quality of 50-year-old Don's sperm was the problem. The risk of miscarriage triples for fathers who are thirty-five or older compared to fathers who are under twenty-five. The same applies to the Delayer's worries about Down Syndrome—it turns out increasing age in men, as in women, ups the risk.

It gets worse. Compared to children born to dads under age 30, kids born to fathers over 40 have six times the risk of autism. For dads over fifty, the risk increases ten-fold. Some researchers believe that the recent increase in autism spectrum disorders is, at least partially, due to the increasing number of older dads. Thanks to long overdue research, the list of worrisome effects connected to paternal age continues to grow. In addition to miscarriage, Down Syndrome, and autism, these include, in no particular order: premature birth, early-onset bipolar disorder, birth defects, cleft palate, water on the brain, dwarfism, progeria, neurofibromatosis, Marfan syndrome, prostate and other cancers, decreased intellectual capacity, and schizophrenia.

If you find this surprising, join the group. Even we, a developmental psychologist and a biologist, only got wind of these paternal effects in recent years. How can this be? There are two reasons. First, the research on dad's age has lagged considerably behind comparable studies on mom's age effects. To put it sarcastically, it is amazing how problems are not detected when no research is conducted. Or, even more sarcastically, it is amazing how problems are not detected when we assume that women—but not men—could cause them.

Second, although there has been a significant push recently in the research on paternal effects, the findings have not been widely discussed or disseminated. For instance, doctors and even genetic counselors are not in the habit of mentioning them to couples trying to conceive. The exception is Down Syndrome. In this case, parents-to-be can go through prenatal diagnosis and make decisions about how to proceed. But there are no prenatal tests for autism or schizophrenia, and the other genetic disorders are very rare and so it is probably considered impractical to test for all of them. Someday we may be able to test a man's sperm to see if he is at risk for a particular disorder. As it stands, the only option is to tell couples about the risks, which isn't happening. The charitable interpretation of this reticence is that doctors feel that it is unkind to cause anxiety when there is nothing much that can be done.

But there is something that can be done. We can spread the word and couples can use this information to make informed reproductive decisions.

WHY DOES AGE MATTER?

If natural selection designs organisms to survive and successfully reproduce, why is human reproduction so vulnerable to chromosomal and genetic mishaps? The answer is that sexual reproduction is ridiculously complicated. (At the cellular level, at least; at the behavioral level, it may just be a matter of dim lighting and a bottle of wine...see chapter 6.)

In older parents, the eggs and sperm cells that must come together are...well...older. Recall that a woman is born with all the eggs she will ever have. Once puberty is reached, one of these eggs will be selected to mature and be ovulated. So, a 38-year-old woman has eggs that have lived with her for 38 years. They have experienced much of what she has—both the good and the bad. Consequently, an older woman has had more time for damage to her

DNA to occur. As we've seen, because her eggs are older, an older woman's cells are also less agile at dividing properly; this causes chromosomal abnormalities.

Things are a bit different, but also risky, in an older man. Once a guy reaches puberty, the processes of creating new sperm and maturing existing sperm are always taking place. That makes it seem like there should be fewer risks for older men compared to older women. But, as we've seen, there are plenty of risks associated with older dads. Why? In addition to having older germ cells, as older women do compared to younger women, older men have another disadvantage. An older man has sperm cells that have gone through countless rounds of division. Just as in the child's game of telephone, the more replications the original material undergoes, the more likely there are to be mistakes in the final version.

EPIGENETICS

There's another category of issues that arise with age. What turns one gene on and another one off? What makes it so that one gene is made at really high levels while another is not? This is the stuff of the relatively new field of *epigenetics*, which studies how experience changes our cells. When our cells are hit with a toxin or other environmental insult, the DNA may become damaged. Sometimes our bodies can repair the damage and sometimes they can't. Sometimes, changes to the DNA occur that turn on or turn off particular genes. This is another reason why age matters. Over time, more changes both to the genes themselves and to the areas of DNA that control the genes may accumulate in the egg and sperm.

Scientists are just beginning to understand what it takes to leave an epigenetic mark that can turn genes on or off. This developing field of epigenetics is yielding insights into what was previously observed, but not explained. We now know that as we age we acquire more epigenetic markers. Think of an epigenetic marker as a tag on top of the genes—*epi* means above—that controls their expression. It's like parental controls for TV: the stations and TV shows still exist, but they can't be turned on. Problems also occur in the other direction, when epigenetic markers turn on genes that are supposed to be turned off. This can affect the likelihood of conception, and may also partly explain the higher incidence of miscarriage with increased age. Stay tuned, we are likely to see important new discoveries in the near future. Already, one research group has shown that the consistency or inconsistency of food availability of grandparents affected the overall health of their grandchildren—this appears to be an epigenetic effect.

If our method of reproduction is so prone to genetic mishaps, then why did it ever evolve? Logically, there must be some compensating advantage for sex to make evolutionary sense...

WHY SEX?

And so now, we must turn to the ultimate answer to the ultimate odd behavior question: What joker came up with sexual intercourse as the way to make a baby, anyway? On the one hand, we don't really care. We like it. Why ask penetrating questions? On the other hand, considered for a few seconds—human copulation does seem to be a bizarre tangle of legs, arms, and other appendages.

From an evolutionary perspective, the mystery becomes even deeper. The "joker" that designed sex is, of course, natural selection itself. The question is: why would natural selection invent sex when there were already other perfectly good methods of reproduction around? Before sexual reproduction came on the scene, billions of years ago other creatures passed copies of their genes to descendants by dividing, or by budding off replicas of themselves (as in yeast) or underground stems, for instance.

Non-sexual reproduction is still common today and it has two distinct advantages compared to sex. First, it allows individuals to pass down 100 percent of their genes to their descendants, whereas our way of "doing it" only transmits half of our genes into future generations—the other half comes from our mate. Second, non-sexual reproduction is simpler. Think of all the time and energy that humans devote to seeking a mate and advertising themselves as potential mates, not to mention the frequent copulation that is necessary to get a female with concealed ovulation pregnant. All this extra time and trouble, for only half the genetic payoff!

And yet sexual reproduction has been around for billions of years and currently does the job for a wide variety of species. It must have something going for it—but what? The most likely explanation is this:

Sex Fights Germs.

We know, we know. It sounds like a commercial for mouthwash. Not only that, but it sounds downright unintuitive considering our modern preoccupation with the germ *spreading* nature of sex through sexually transmitted diseases. But this is the current leading theory. It is called the Red Queen hypothesis, and it makes a lot of sense.

The fact is: we humans are under attack! There are viruses, bacteria and even things called prions that cause Mad Cow Disease, that are always figuring out new ways to infect, reproduce and get themselves transmitted to other carriers. To infect, reproduce, and so on...

The life cycle of some of these simple organisms is very short; some bacteria, for instance, live for about 30 minutes. Even in that short time, they can reproduce like crazy. What this means is that natural selection works very quickly on these buggers; they can change characteristics in almost no time at all. This is a big advantage for the germs. That means that we need to keep shuffling our own genetic deck if we are to stay one step ahead of the germs. And of course the germs themselves are constantly changing in response to our genetic reshuffling. Consequently, we humans have to "run to stay in the same place," as Lewis Carroll's Red Queen says to Alice in *Through the Looking-Glass*.

And that, in fact, is what sex allows us to do. Scientists believe that sexual reproduction evolved because it promotes a constant reshuffling of genes.

For humans the story becomes really interesting when we consider an intricate protein complex that plays a critical role in the immune system. This protein, called the Major Histocompatibility Complex (MHC), provides a kind of scaffolding mirror image match to the kinds of bugs our bodies may encounter. The MHC must recognize an invader for our bodies to mount an effective response—an effective immune system must "know its enemies." By coming up with a lot of different combinations in your MHCs you can fight off lots of different bugs. For this reason, the ideal situation for your future offspring is to reproduce with someone whose MHC proteins are really different from yours. That would give your child an advantage in fighting off illness. But how can you identify whose MHC molecules are different from yours? Do you need to swab cheeks on the first date and send the samples off to a lab?

Nope. Biology has done it for you. It turns out that you are naturally attracted to folks whose MHC molecules differ from your own; you prefer their scents and rate them as sexier than members of the opposite sex who have MHCs that are similar to your own. You don't even have to think about it or take a genetics course; biology has solved the problem for you. So when you feel that there is real chemistry between you and a potential mate, this is likely to be true—literally!!!

And so sex became useful in the fight against germs. In a constantly changing environment, different combinations of certain genes may yield competitive advantages that promote survival. By creating offspring who are always genetically different, sex made it harder for parasites to find a way around our bodies' defenses. In effect, sexual reproduction allowed us to develop a vast array of potential responses to germs. These germs may treat us like homes, but they are less likely to get the run of the house because the house's burglar alarm/defense system is changing with every new person they inhabit.

BABIES WITHOUT SEX

As we write this, the real-life Deborah has a few more months to go before she has her baby. Let's keep our fingers crossed. We don't know if Deb and Don have used any of the currently available methods of prenatal diagnosis to determine if their baby-to-be has Down's syndrome or some other medical problem. Nor do we know what they would do if this were the case. If they did make the painful decision to terminate the pregnancy, or if Deb miscarried again, will the Delayers have missed out on the chance to become parents?

No. One option would be to adopt a baby. Adoption is interesting from an evolutionary perspective. You might think that nature could not possibly have built parents that could fall in love with and care for a baby that does not carry their genes. But you would be wrong. As research and reports from adults who were adopted as infants show, relationships between parents and adopted infants are indistinguishable from those of parents and offspring they give birth to. These babies are at least as likely to grow up and lead happy, well-adjusted lives as babies raised by their genetic parents. This makes a lot of sense, actually. Just as natural selection has designed adults to desire sex whether or not it actually leads to the birth of a child carrying our genes, it has designed parents so that they readily become emotionally attached to a baby in their care. In the ancient past, such a child would virtually always have been theirs biologically as well.

Because the availability of healthy babies has declined, more people are adopting from foreign countries or taking children who are older or who have developmental problems. As you would expect, the disadvantages that some of these kids have faced can lead to challenges for parents and children alike. But despite having had stressful early lives these children fare surprisingly well.

One reason must surely be that, like the Delayers, adoptive parents usually have higher than average incomes, which in our society provides access to all kind of things, including access to better healthcare. In addition, adoptive parents are typically so thrilled to be able to have a child that they become excellent, responsive parents.

Deborah and Donald have another option. Having taken advantage of birth control methods for years in order to have sex without children, they might now use modern reproductive technology to have a child without having sex! Donor insemination ("artificial insemination"), *in vitro* fertilization (IVF or "test tube babies"), and surrogate motherhood aim at helping couples who have decided not to risk pregnancy because of a history of genetic disease, or who are among the one-sixth of all couples that discover that they are sterile. Deb and Don could try *in vitro* fertilization, for instance. In this procedure, Deb would be given some hormones that stimulate the ripening of several eggs at once. These would then be removed surgically and placed in a dish of nutrients, to which Don's sperm could be added. After the eggs are fertilized, a small number would be injected back into Deb's uterus, where, with luck, one would implant and develop into a baby.

What if it's too late for IVF, because Deb's eggs are just too old? No problem! The amazing truth is that Deb can wait 20 more years if she wants to. Today, a woman can actually give birth after menopause. (Perhaps in that case Deb and Don would have to change their last name to "Superdelayer".) All that's needed is a donor egg from a younger woman combined with the in vitro fertilization procedure just described. Keep in mind, though, this strategy is associated with a number of additional risks.

SURELY YOU JEST

These days, starting a family when you're fairly young is easier said than done. There are some serious tradeoffs to consider. Here again, as throughout the book, we find a mismatch between evolution and how we currently live. So what should we do? It does seem wise for both women *and* men to try to have kids while in their twenties.

Hard to do. But if we work to change attitudes about parenthood in the workplace, perhaps it could become more feasible.

Chapter 5

WHY PEOPLE MATTER MORE
THAN MONEY

*I am without the man I married...Where will I see the food that will help
my children grow? Who is going to help me raise this newborn?*
                                              -Nisa, a !Kung San hunter-gatherer woman

It takes a village.

                                                                    -African proverb

A true story:

Gloria Graduate

An unmarried 22-year-old woman just out of college yearns for a child
of her own. She begins having unprotected sex with her new boyfriend,
whose drinking problem is becoming more and more apparent. One year later
she has a beautiful baby girl of her own and has married the father. But in the
meantime her husband's drinking has gotten out of control and within months
she files for a divorce. She earns a small but steady income by doing
consulting on the internet, which allows her to work in her suburban home.
She also gets additional economic support from her parents.

Compared to Deborah Delayer, Gloria has all the advantages of youth on
her side. She is at the peak of her fertility—this occurs in the early twenties for
well-fed populations like her own–and finds it quite easy to get pregnant. Her
chances of giving birth to a child with genetic abnormalities, or Down's
syndrome or other chromosomal disorders are very low. She is also doing fine
in the resources department. Unlike the vast majority of single moms, who

struggle financially and are often very poor, Gloria lives quite comfortably because she has a supplemental income from her parents.

Although she has youth and resources on her side, you might wonder whether Gloria's prospects for a happy family life with her daughter are as great as they could be. On the one hand, the notion that Gloria needs a man to be happy sounds dangerously outdated, laughably so. On the other hand, wouldn't a single dad be in the same less-than-happy boat? The question really is this: is it better to have a committed co-parent than to raise a child as a single parent?

From a Darwinian perspective, perhaps the most incredible thing about Gloria's situation is that it is even survivable. Hannah Hunter-gatherer and her baby would not have been able to survive without hubby Harold and her social group. As with our sex lives, we live in a time of greater than ever choice in composing a family. That's a wonderful thing. But the fact that raising kids alone is possible financially does not make it easy, even in these days of supermarket foraging. To understand why single parenting is tough, we need to consider the evolution of two great human universals: romantic love and trust.

WHY PEOPLE EVERYWHERE FALL IN LOVE: THE ANCIENT TWO-PARENT ADVANTAGE

Believe it or not, scholars once claimed that love was "socially constructed"; that is to say, a 12th century invention that occurs only in some cultures. But when evolutionary-minded anthropologists checked to see if this was true, they found that, on the contrary, romantic love occurs everywhere. So if anyone tries to tell you that love is an unusual behavior invented by the troubadours and is just a Western or European thing, you can tell them that they need to keep up with the research. Love is universal!

Not only that, but the vast majority of men and women in most human societies end up in long-term relationships that other members of the society recognize as a sort of contract. This couple has sex repeatedly, mainly or exclusively with each other. When there are babies, both partners—males and females—are expected to provide care for their children.

Of course there are exceptions. There are societies in which a prosperous male may have more than one wife. But, if you look into it a bit it becomes clear that these are the exceptions that prove the rule. Big harems only became possible late in human evolution when a few men were able to concentrate great wealth; they are not even close to being universal. The human design seems to be for pairing off. You might argue that "one-night stands" are an exception to our tendency to seek long-term partners. But many species have *nothing but* one-night stands, while we humans also typically engage in many-year and even many-decade stands: as we write this, Linc's parents are celebrating their 60th anniversary! Thus, humans tend to engage in what is called "serial monogamy"—a tendency to have a series of long-term committed relationships. This term captures our predilection for marriage, but also dating before marriage and the fact that most folks get remarried after divorce.

There are a couple of other universals worth mentioning. Human fathers provide for their offspring. We all know that there can be huge differences in the amount of parental care provided by moms and dads, which in many ways is cultural. Moms usually do more. Even so, the anthropological record is clear: most kids get care from their father as well, in the form of some child care, teaching, protection, and provision of food and shelter. We evolved to be co-parents.

Finally, the traits that we seek in a prospective mate are also universal. Whatever people's distinct tastes in long-term partners may be, research across many different cultures has shown that all over the globe men and women share a desire for a long-term mate who has certain qualities. In addition to wanting someone who is as attracted to us as we are to them, humans all seek mates who are intelligent, kind, and dependable.

Why would natural selection ever do us the favor of designing us for love? For entering into long-term relationships? For seeking a smart, kind, dependable long-term partner that is attracted to us? The answer is simple: because dual parenting worked better than single parenting as a way of keeping ancient hunter-gatherer children alive. Kids are a lot of work! They are born helpless and are entirely dependent on others for their survival.

Ancient hunter-gatherer mothers spent a significant amount of time finding and preparing food, typically while carrying the baby and carrying or supervising an ancient "preschooler"! Given the burdens of 40 weeks of pregnancy, four years of breastfeeding at frequent intervals, and the overall arduous nature of an ancient mom's existence, it is easy to see why single motherhood would not have been a viable lifestyle for Hannah Hunter-gatherer.

The cold truth is that in hunter-gatherer times, not having a second parent to help out was potentially fatal for a child. As a result, natural selection came up with a brilliant design solution to the problem of how to keep both parents around to care for a child: love. At first it's the sizzling, passionate, "I-just-want-to-be-by-your-side" emotion of love; this often turns into a "we have created a life together" companionate kind of love. And you thought evolution just gave us bad stuff, like hate and aggression! Thankfully, it also gave us love.

Of course, today, single motherhood or single fatherhood is survivable for both parent and child if, like Gloria, you have a dependable income. The trouble is that single parenthood *used to* threaten the survival of parent and child. You may not feel sorry for Gloria at all, given her lucrative family connection. She lives in a comfortable house in a suburb and even has a disposable income, which she uses on home decor, an assortment of pets, and other frills of 21st century upper-middle class living. Gloria herself may even be inclined to argue that she and her daughter will survive just fine, thank you very much. But she also says that she often feels unhappy. Why?

These unpleasant feelings exist because they motivated a hunter-gatherer mom who lost a husband to death or desertion to *do something* to change her circumstances, thus increasing her kids' chances of survival. Lacking day to day social contact, Gloria's mind may be sending her a signal that her prospects for successfully raising her child are in jeopardy—even though, in today's world, this isn't true.

This is why even though financially, she's fine, Gloria's prospects for a truly happy life are more limited than they could have been. A partner would be nice. But Gloria's problem is not simply the lack of a committed long-term partner. It's the lack of *any* supportive social network.

It Takes a Village

Like all of us, Gloria is built for survival in an ancient hunter-gatherer environment, and that included more than just predators, prey, husbands and kids. It included a fair number of *other people* as well. We are, perhaps above all else, social creatures. Our ancient ancestors didn't pair off as husband and wife and then live in a little hut by themselves. They lived alongside other couples and family relations with whom they shared territory and cooperated in the daily tasks of hunter-gatherer living. Estimates of the size of ancient hunter-gatherer groups range from 30 to 150; many or most of these people would have been related to each other. An important feature of these groups was the daily intimate contact that occurred between the members. Everyone knew the neighbors.

What's more, the neighbors helped care for the kids. Wherever reasonably safe child care options were available, hunter-gatherer moms made use of them, as parents do today. Leaving a baby with an aunt, grandmother, or someone else in one's group made it possible for mom to go forage alone, bathe, or tend to her toddler. Evolutionary-minded scientists call these alternative caregivers "alloparents."

WHY HUMANS NEED ALLOPARENTS: OUR HELPLESS, ALTRICIAL, BEAUTIFUL BUT CHALLENGING BABIES

Have you ever watched a video of a foal standing up for the first time, minutes after birth? Scientists would characterize that type of development as "precocious," in contrast to "altricial" or slow development. Consider baby chicks, an altricial species. At the Boston Museum of Science, one can watch chicks hatch. Even these little birds, the epitome of an animal whose young requires extensive parental investment, are up and on their feet within hours.

It will take *your* baby *a year* to walk! Your baby is going to be super altricial.

Not only are humans born helpless, they remain dependent on others for a very, very long time compared to every other species. This means that the parental effort (often called "parental investment") required to keep a baby alive during the first year of life is enormous. It gets a bit less intense after that, but it still takes several years before one can, for instance, comfortably leave a child unattended—even in a protected environment like a home or fenced-in yard.

Given the altricial nature of our young'uns, how is it possible that ancient hunter-gatherers ever had more than one child? Given the investment required, wouldn't siblings have to be at least six or seven years apart? Anthropologist Sarah Blaffer Hrdy points to the importance of alloparents, these other individuals who help the primary parent.

Who are these alloparents? Typically, they are related to the baby. In many primate species, including humans, alloparents include female relatives as well: typically, the maternal grandmother, but also the aunts, older sisters, or cousins of the baby.

Why do the baby's relatives, other than mom and dad, help with the infant care? Evolutionary biologists call helping behavior that is directed toward one's biological relatives "kin altruism." The basic idea is that people help their biological relatives because they carry copies of the same genes. Kin altruism exists because natural selection is really—strictly speaking—about the spreading of genes. Genes can be thought of as the instructions that build the brain that guides the behavior of the person. Genes that build a brain that produces behavior that promotes the survival and reproduction of copies of themselves will tend to spread in the population. This is the modern, updated version of evolutionary theory. It is a bit hard to grasp at first, but is quite a powerful tool for understanding social behavior and family dynamics. It's called *kin selection* theory.

WHY DOES MOM HATE HER MOTHER-IN-LAW?

Consider this alloparenting factoid: in certain non-human primates, the rate of death of the first-born offspring is dramatically reduced by the presence of the maternal grandmother. Hrdy and others have long noted that the primate maternal grandmothers are a tremendous boon for their grandchildren. (Recall the grandmother hypothesis discussed in chapter 4.)

What about the paternal grandmother? We need only think in evolutionary terms to take the sting out of this sentiment that resonates with so many women. One clue to the answer is that kin altruism involving infant care almost always occurs among *females*. And only certain females. Why should this be so?

The maternal grandmother knows beyond a doubt that her grandbaby is biologically related to her. Heck, the egg that created that grandbaby began its life in the grandmother's body during the fetal development of the mother. The baby popped out of her daughter. But the situation is different for the paternal grandmother—the grandbaby didn't come out of her son's body. Just as fathers might somewhere in a dark moment question their own baby's paternity—even if such "cheating" is unlikely to have occurred—the paternal grandmother can never be 100% certain that the grandbaby is hers. Consequently, evolutionary biologists argue, she is not as inclined to provide help for the grandchild.

For the father of the baby, the in-law situation is different. When the mom and dad were dating, the mother-in-law-to-be probably had a lot to say about her prospective son-in-law. In this case, it matters much more during the dating part of the relationship because it is in her genes' interests to have her daughter's mate be of the highest possible genetic quality. Good paternal genes would mean both good genes for the baby, and good provisioning on the part of the baby's father. So, if she is not impressed with her daughter's beau, this might cause some initial tension between dad and maternal grandma.

Once the baby is born, though, things change. Now, all dad's mother-in-law really wants her daughter's mate to do is to help protect and "provision" or provide food for her grandchildren. She doesn't really care if he is the biological father or not, because this does not affect the spreading of her own genes—those are unequivocally residing in her daughter's baby. So, once the baby arrives, the maternal grandmother often "comes to the rescue"—whether or not she had really liked the baby's father or not to begin with.

What about grandfathers? We all know wonderful, loving grandfathers. But evolutionary logic dictates that in general, on average, they will be less invested in their grandchildren than a maternal grandmother. Think it through. If the "father" cannot be 100% sure that his wife's offspring are biologically his, then this is also true for the next generation out. So, if grandpa helps less with the infant care than grandma does, kin selection theory provides a scientific explanation, but not an excuse!

We realize that this kin selection theory stuff may sound harsh to the reader. In some ways, it's just not very pleasant to think about—even though it explains a lot! Keep in mind, however, that these biases in helping behavior are not conscious. It's more that nature builds all of us with a slight "push" in a certain direction—in general, on average, the less certain the biological relationship, the less investment. Of course, many other factors also affect helping behavior.

THE EVOLUTION OF TRUST

The opportunity for making use of alloparents was surely one of the reasons that humans evolved to live in social groups. Alloparenting feels pretty natural (and necessary!) to modern day moms, but it is actually rare among nonhuman primates. Many primate mothers will just not leave their babies with other females. Consequently, these species have fewer offspring than humans are designed to have. In contrast, careful study of one modern-day hunter-gatherer tribe showed that women typically had seven or eight offspring. Humans are built to have lots of babies, even though we no longer do—thanks to the advent of vasectomies and hormonal birth control. If you doubt that humans "naturally" have many offspring, think about how many siblings your great-grandparents had.

All of which brings us back to our question: given the altricial nature of human infants, how on earth was it possible for Hannah and Harold hunter-gatherer to have seven or eight kids?! To really spread one's genes, the most prolific strategy is obviously to have many offspring. If our babies were fast-maturing, we could just keep pushing them out—soon, our baby would be able to fend for itself and we could have another one. This is the pattern that much of nature shows us. But, no...*our* babies take *forever* to fend for themselves. Which is why humans are able to grow our impressive, adaptable, experience-tuned brains.

Sarah Blaffer Hrdy argues that the evolution of *the ability to trust "others" with our offspring* was a crucial precursor to the distinctive kind of human family life that we know today. In many other species, though, a female will harm or neglect a newborn that is not their own—even if they are related. In humans, at some point, trust evolved. An ancient woman who had the capacity to trust family with her helpless, altricial, beautiful but challenging baby, could soon have another helpless, altricial, beautiful but challenging baby. In early humans, nearby females were almost always directly related to the baby. Like romantic love, trust is a beautiful adaptation that is at the heart of the nature of our species.

MOTHER COLLEAGUES

As we've seen, in most cases, alloparents are kin. Women trust their biological relatives to help with the care of their baby. But here again, we have a mismatch in the way we evolved and the way we live. Most of us simply do not live near kin. And for those of us who do, we typically don't have as many aunts, cousins, etc. nearby as our ancestors once did. So how are we to raise these helpless, altricial, beautiful but challenging babies?

Moms depend on their mom friends, other mothers who have children the same age as one's own children. These "mother colleagues" are analogous to modern-day work colleagues. Work colleagues remind each other about important deadlines, meetings and conferences; mother colleagues remind each other about soccer sign-ups, registrations, and school open-houses. Work colleagues share responsibility for projects; mother colleagues organize carpools, sleepovers and parties. Work colleagues jump in when we are sick or on vacation; mother colleagues trade daycare, so they can each volunteer in their children's classes at school. Work colleagues often collaborate when projects need to be completed or when problems arise; mother colleagues discuss issues at school to help work out a resolution.

Our work colleagues are people whose work we respect, and who we trust will not undermine us or steal credit for our work. These relationships build over time. Similarly, mother colleagues typically have similar parenting styles and respect each other's rules. They don't undermine our own parenting beliefs or promote competition between their children and ours. These relationships, too, are built over time. Without trusted colleagues at work, most of us would be unable to perform our jobs as expected. Without trusted mother colleagues, moms would not be able to have more than one dependent child at a time.

Hillary Clinton famously titled a book with the African proverb, "it takes a village." This phrase is understood—and lived—in virtually every part of the world. Even so, a famous retort attracted much attention: "... it does not take a village to raise a child. It takes a family to raise a child." This clearly resonated with certain voters. Why? Anyone who cares for children knows how labor-intensive the job is. Did the individual making the statement, and those who agreed with it, have very little to do with the day-to-day ins and outs of raising their own children? Part of the answer may be that—largely for historical reasons—we are more likely in the USA than in other cultures to think of the nuclear family as a somewhat independent economic entity. Of course, as soon as you look around a bit in our country, and to other cultures, you quickly see the remnants of social and economic interdependence that characterized ancient human family life. You can see bits and pieces of this social connectedness everywhere in daily life—in school buses, public schools, libraries, pediatricians' offices, and supermarkets.

Can you feel the political tension here? It derives, we would suggest, from a classic evolutionary mismatch between our evolved human design and the modern world we live in. The socially connected life that humans are designed for is at odds with the more socially and economically separate nature of family life in the modern US. *Of course* families are central in human childrearing. As we've seen, kin selection theory makes this quite clear. But those who are directly involved in their children's care know that it takes more—a village, or a modern day surrogate of a village. Alloparenting is an ancient human universal. When we don't have kin around to help, we look to other parents with children of the same age, our mother colleagues. Without this assistance, raising a family becomes very difficult indeed.

Where does all this leave Gloria? Evolutionary-minded writers have suggested that the loneliness and "alienation" of modern living is due to the fact that we no longer live in groups of individuals that are truly dependent on each other. This is perhaps most obvious in the suburbs, where—like many suburbanites—Gloria lives in an isolated house carefully set apart from her neighbors, whom she hardly knows. She can come home from foraging at the supermarket and, using her garage door opener, enter directly into her house without even having to acknowledge the person taking out the garbage next door. And since her child is not yet in school, she doesn't have any mother colleagues. Yet. Cross your fingers for her.

Gloria is fortunate in one respect. She realized early on—despite the dubious claims sometimes promulgated in the media—that it was very difficult to get her work done while taking caring of a baby at home. Because of the second income she receives from her parents, Gloria can afford to drop her daughter off at a small, home-based day care center. So she has good, reliable daycare, unlike many. Good daycare can be viewed as one modern-day version of alloparenting.

Overall, it seems that Gloria may have made a mistake when she rather impulsively decided to start a family with a troubled mate in an untested relationship. Which leads to another question. If we are built to seek high quality mates, why did Gloria choose such a loser? We may never know the complete answer. But Gloria's behavior is not inconsistent with the research cited, since that work is concerned with the qualities that people say they would like to have in an *ideal* mate. Peoples' *actual* mate choices are always limited to the available pool of potential mates, of course. Since she knew relatively few available men at the time, Gloria's mate choice is perhaps somewhat less mysterious—but no less costly in terms of her own happiness.

MISMATCHES AND TRADEOFFS

Let's take a minute to review the family planning decisions made by Deborah and Donald Delayer and by Gloria Graduate. In both cases, these modern parents took advantage of choices that were not available to our hunter-gatherer ancestors—exploiting the mismatch between ancient and modern living. But in doing so, they had to make some tradeoffs. They each had to trade greater freedom of choice for something that Hannah and Harold the Hunter-gatherers had as they started their family lives.

The Delayers delayed. Deborah in particular traded *youth* for extra time to remain single, find a truly desirable mate, and pursue her career. As a result, the Delayers ran some risks and experienced some setbacks. If their good luck continues, however, they will soon have a healthy child. If they are less lucky, they may face the mixed blessing of raising a child with a disorder—not the end of the world, but not what they are hoping for.

Gloria traded *people* for the opportunity to have a child when she wanted one. She chose to conceive before she had a reliable co-parent to help her out and in the absence of other forms of social support. Partly because of her impulsive choice of a mate and partly because of the isolating effects of modern suburbs, Gloria's day-to-day life is a bit of an emotional struggle, a little empty. She could be happier.

In modern life, it's not easy to be young *and* in a well-established relationship *and* financially secure when you start a family. It's simply not possible to completely control these aspects of our lives. Had Deborah settled for the wrong husband in order to have a child earlier, she could be in Gloria's position. Had Gloria waited for the right guy to come along she could be in Deborah and Donald's position, or she may never have had a child at all.

And let's not forget that both the Delayers and Gloria had the good sense to postpone parenthood until they had adequate *resources*. But how much is adequate? The answer may surprise you.

How Much Does a Baby Cost?

Yet another true story:

Lisa and Lyel Lovebird

A woman and man fall in love at age 20 while in college. They immediately start living together and grow closer through many shared experiences, including a few serious arguments. Five years later they move to another state, get married, and are just starting on the long road to establishing themselves in their respective careers. Although it feels to them that they are just barely making ends meet, and they have no guarantees that they will be making a lot more money in the near future, they have their first child three years later at age 28.

The Lovebirds certainly are no spring chickens by hunter-gatherer standards, but they are doing okay age-wise (youth).

They also have a well-tested and enduring relationship (people). The fact that they have each other is also an economic advantage, of course. Single motherhood is especially difficult financially. Consider:

- Having a child is the best predictor that a woman will end up in financial collapse
- single moms are more likely than any other group to file for bankruptcy–more likely than the elderly, more likely than divorced men, and more likely than people living in poor neighborhoods
- single moms who have been to college are actually 60% more likely to end up bankrupt than their less educated single sisters

Gender inequities in pay are clearly a huge part of the problem for single moms. One recent analysis reported that of 265 careers, women were paid less than men in 264 of them. How much of a discrepancy is there? On average women earn 77 cents for every dollar that their comparable male colleagues earn. To worsen matters, when children are young, many women tend to work low-wage jobs, perhaps under the impression that they will allow for a flexible schedule. In fact, this is usually not the case. For these women, the financial impact is immediate and continues into retirement, leading to low retirement savings and limited social security.

So the Lovebirds are an economic team and that is promising. Like many couples, however, their current net worth (resources) is virtually nil and they are uncertain about their future prospects—will they both get decent jobs that pay enough to support a family? Should they have waited to start their family?

Trying to figure out when you can afford a baby is tough. Among the unsolicited pieces of advice you may receive is that "If you wait for the perfect time, you'll never have kids." That is certainly true. On the other hand, just scraping by sounds stressful.

In a study conducted by the USDA for data from 2012, the average cost to raise a child is $241,080. If that seems oddly low to you, it's because that does not include the cost of college! That's just what it takes to raise a child until they are 18 years old. That average varies dramatically depending on where you live. In the urban Northeast, it takes $446,100 to raise a child to 18 years of age; in a rural area, it takes $143,160. Regional differences in the cost of housing and daycare contribute to this variability. For example, the average cost of daycare for an infant in Mississippi is $4,600; in Massachusetts, it's $15, 000! (How much money do you have to net to make a 15K daycare cost seem reasonable?)

Of course, these numbers are just for raising one child. If you want to play around with the math, the USDA provides a calculator for estimating the cost of your hypothetical child or children: www.cnpp.usda.gov/calculatorintro. htm. For many couples, this website may also serve as a great form of birth control!

But then, even before money was invented it was expensive to have a kid. Because they are so altricial, babies "cost" a lot. You have to keep supporting them well after the time when they are babies. For Hannah and Harold Hunter-gatherer, the cost of providing for a kid from birth to independence was something like 10 to 13 million calories, not counting the food an older child could collect for herself. No foraging woman could gather that much herself, but by the time Hannah was capable of having a child she had become an expert in the skills necessary to support herself and could provide much of the food necessary to support a child. With the addition of a second "income" from Harold, the couple could support both themselves and a child. Whether this was relatively easy or excruciatingly difficult depended on local conditions.

Alas, as always, things are more complicated today. In a complex technological society like ours, Lisa and Lyel needed an *education* in order to get *jobs* to make enough *money* to support themselves and their child, unless of course they wanted to revert to a hunter-gatherer lifestyle (they didn't). This education took so long to acquire, in fact, that it extended well past the age at which they became reproductively mature. As a result, Lisa and Lyel waited quite a bit longer to start their family than Hannah and Harold Hunter-gatherer did. However, the Lovebirds have only a bare bones income and the hope that their college degrees will lead to a better financial future. Wouldn't they be happier if they waited even longer?

The surprising answer is no. As Darwin-inspired psychologist Timothy Miller puts it in his 1994 book, *How to Want What You Have*—perhaps the first evolutionary self-help book ever: "It is human nature always to want a little more. People spend their lives honestly believing that they have almost enough of whatever they want. Just a little more will put them over the top; then they will be contented forever." Research conducted in the two decades since the publication of Miller's book strongly supports his thesis: No matter how much we have, we all continue to desire more. Why?

As Miller points out, only evolutionary theory can make sense of such a bizarre human trait. An ancient hunter-gatherer person who was easily satisfied with the resources they had would usually end up having less than someone who always wanted a little more. The latter person would, in turn, tend to be more reproductively successful.

What's more, a large body of research supports Miller's other central thesis: beyond a certain minimal income, making more money just doesn't make people any happier. And so, we are built to yearn for more. But getting more doesn't make us happier. People tend, on average, to say that they are pretty happy—regardless of their income.

This is all a bit tragic. The implication seems to be that none of us will ever be completely satisfied with our level of prosperity. We will always think of ourselves as pretty happy, but we will always yearn for more. But wait. It gets worse. How do we know what to yearn for? The embarrassing truth is that we are built to gauge our own desires by observing what other people have. We not only yearn, we yearn for what others have but we do not. This is not a big problem in societies where everyone has a similar standard of living. People are much less satisfied in societies with vast class differences. What this means is that unless you are very rich, a part of you will always be hankering for more. Thus it is that our evolutionary heritage cons us into 60 hour work weeks and inevitably makes us feel guilty when we cannot provide our children with all their little heart's desire. And kid's hearts, like our own, always desire more.

Miller devotes most of his book to describing strategies to help us keep our relentless desire for more in check. For our present purposes, though, the main point is this: Hunter-gatherers frequently had enough resources to support a child. Otherwise we wouldn't be here. And what did they have? By our modern standards, almost nothing! Yet the modern day hunter-gatherers that have been studied don't live their lives in the depths of depression. Similarly, by hunter-gatherer standards people today—even poor people today—live in conditions of unimaginable wealth, comfort, and security. Yet no one is walking around in ecstasy because of this. Most people throughout human existence have probably been fairly satisfied with their lot, whatever it was, but thought that just a little bit more would make them happier.

If you believe all this, as we do, what sort of advice would *you* give couples trying to decide whether or not to wait to have children? Go for it! Right? The only problem is if the couples actually take your advice. If they do, then they may come back and say, "You told us to go ahead and have kids, but now our lives are really difficult. We are not that happy. If only we had waited until we made more money, we would be so much happier." But they would be missing the whole point. Happiness is simply not strongly influenced by wealth. The disgruntled couple is wrong: if they had waited for a bigger paycheck before having children, chances are their level of happiness would be about the same. But that's not the way it feels: when you are built to yearn, you are going to yearn, no matter what.

And so we will stick our necks out and say to you: If you have a bare bones but reasonably steady income—or possibly even just the prospect of such an income—and you want a child, by all means, Go For It! Just don't come back to us later complaining that you wish you had waited until you had more money.

TAKE-HOME MESSAGE FROM CHAPTERS 4 AND 5

Given what we've said about evolution, the Delayers, Gloria Graduate, and the Lovebirds, a good rule of thumb for modern family planning—something to shoot for, anyway—would be to start:

- *before* a woman hits her 40s and preferably quite a bit earlier, but only
- *after* establishing an enduring relationship with a desirable co-parent or, lacking that, a strong network of social support, and
- *after* establishing a steady income or the prospects for one; surprisingly, even a very modest wage by modern standards will do.

Of course, parenthood is *survivable* even if you don't have all of these things—or any of them, for that matter. None of the people described in the scenarios in this chapter are leading horrific lives. All the same, starting out with this simple threesome is going make a big difference as you face the many parenting challenges ahead.

Like getting pregnant.

PART III. TAKING THE PLUNGE

If parenting is a long distance swim, then pregnancy is the exciting time when you have just taken the plunge. Brace yourself—what with pregnancy sickness, difficulty sleeping, and other discomforts, the water may seem a little cold at times. You'll want to do what you can do to have a healthy pregnancy and birth. Birth! Well, birth will be your first exposure to some really strong seas.

How can you promote the formation and growth of your baby-to-be while maintaining your own physical and mental health? What can you do now to make parenting as pleasant and joyful a swim as possible? The purpose of the chapters in this section is to help you make choices that are informed by evolutionary thinking and that work best for you. But first, you're going to have to get pregnant. Ready, set... dive!

- Pardon us for asking, but...do you know how to get pregnant (see Chapter 6)?
- Do you want to change your eating habits while you are pregnant (see Chapters 7 and 8)?
- Are you stressed out (see Chapter 9)?
- What else will you do to get ready for the birth of your baby (see Chapters 10)?

Chapter Sex…er, Six

DIVING IN: A MOSTLY HUMOROUS LOOK AT CONCEIVING

Sex without love is an empty experience.
But as far as empty experiences go, it's one of the best.

-Woody Allen

Let's start at the beginning: why do we have sex?

Well, ok, obviously we have sex because we really, REALLY, like it! But why do we like it so much? Because it is pleasurable, of course. But pleasure is just the obvious, immediate cause of our desiring sex. We can still wonder about the ultimate cause of our desire: why should we find such strange behavior pleasurable? The answer won't surprise you.

The desire for sex is universal. Maleness and femaleness, attraction, arousal: all these pleasurable aspects of life exist because they lead to the creation of babies. To put it another way, sex evolved because it produces some copies of our genes inside a tiny new human, who will grow up before you know it and become a mature human who desires sex!

Not that we are always consciously trying to have children. More often than not, we are really just in it for the sex.

This is an important point. There was no reason for natural selection to design us to consciously try to have children, as long it designed us to do what was necessary to make it happen. Early humans had no idea that their frequent rolls in the savanna hay were connected with the birth of a child forty weeks later. This had to be discovered. No one knows when that happened, but it must have been quite a moment: "You mean when we did…THAT…we made…THIS?!"

Human cultures have recognized the sex-birth connection for a long, long time. Since that momentous discovery, a great many minds over the centuries have devoted enormous resources to working on the problem of how to have sex without making children. Thanks to our great intelligence, we can use modern methods of birth control to enjoy the stone-age pleasures of sex without becoming pregnant.

So, you want to have a baby? Well then, you must now do things as nature intended: you must reestablish the connection between sex and childbirth that you have heretofore severed by using birth control. Your job will not only be pleasant, but also quite easy—or will it?

DR. CRATON'S NOT-SO-SUREFIRE TIPS FOR GETTING PREGNANT

Here are three strategies for getting pregnant:

Strategy #1. Have sex all the time.

Although some couples get pregnant right away using strategy #1, you may be surprised at how long it takes. As I recall, it took my wife and I a full ten months to conceive our son. At the time we had just moved to a modest apartment in the middle of a cornfield, as I started work on a postdoctoral fellowship. My wife decided not to work outside the home during this period. Instead, she put her considerable energy into pursuing two goals: spending a lot of quality time with our firstborn, and making child number two. She succeeded admirably at the difficult task of caring for our 1-year-old daughter in a strange new place, without a lot of daytime help from me. But after several months of trying, we still hadn't made any headway on the second goal. Despite a lot of nighttime help from me.

Personally, I sort of enjoyed our initial lack of success. Birth control can interfere with spontaneity. The beauty of deciding to have children is that for a certain period prospective parents get to forego the anti-child devices and indulge in more spontaneous, whenever-you-want-wherever-you-are sex. If one of you should not happen to be in the mood, the other one can always try to invoke their sense of duty: "I'd also love to watch TV, honey, but don't you think we should work on making that baby?" So I was in no hurry to conceive. What are the chances, I thought, that we'll maintain the same level of sexual activity once we've actually succeeded?

But as weeks turned into months, baby-making became a serious business for my wife. She hoped to get back to work in the not-too-distant future. If she was going to stay at home with a toddler, in the middle of a cornfield, then damn it she was going to get another baby in the oven. Now was the time to conceive. Gradually, the strain of working so hard with so little to show for it drove her a bit crazy. This led to a brief stint with strategy #2.

Strategy #2. Experiment with the various folk remedies you may hear about for pushing the odds more in your favor.

I have no idea if any of these work, and I don't intend to get into it in any detail. But I can say that they make things more interesting. For instance, there is the "get-gravity-to-work-for you" folk remedy. This is the notion that if a husband holds his wife upside-down by the ankles after lovemaking, it will "help keep those boys running upstream" to their destination. And even if it doesn't work, you may still discover a new sense of respect for gymnasts.

My feeling is that if you want to have some fun, keep trying strategy # 2. If you really want a baby soon, though, and strategies 1 and 2 haven't worked for you yet, you may want to supplement them with strategy # 3.

Strategy #3. Try some slightly more scientific approaches for pushing the odds more in your favor.

Related to the "gravity" folk remedy is the more scientific, but only slightly so, "Hoover theory" of female orgasm. The capacity for orgasm is a universal female trait, even if many women find it to be an elusive one. Why did it evolve? It turns out that if a woman has an orgasm soon after her partner does, her uterus contracts in a kind of rhythm that literally sucks the sperm up into her vagina and, possibly, her small intestine (just kidding about the small intestine). This neat trick may have evolved because it allowed ancient women some measure of control over whether the sperm actually makes it to their egg. (Other than not having an orgasm, strategies for not getting pregnant would have included refusing to mate, or standing up after lovemaking—otherwise known as the letting-gravity-work-for-you-in-the-opposite-direction method). Whatever its origins, the vacuum effect of orgasm points couples toward another strategy for getting pregnant: you must practice having your orgasms in quick succession. Practice, practice, practice; even if it doesn't work, you will probably have fun trying.

Another scientific strategy is to try to time your lovemaking to coincide with ovulation. This means determining when there is an egg present to be fertilized, which is about as scientific as predicting the weather. As we saw in chapter 3, menstrual cycles are notoriously irregular—you may recall that the follicular phase of the ovarian cycle, in particular, is quite variable and responds to environmental factors like stress and even the presence of other cycling women. The timing of menstrual cycles also changes over the course of a woman's lifetime. Some women, however, believe they can pinpoint the midpoint of their menstrual cycles based on headaches or other sensations. Maybe! Other methods you might try include using an ovulation test kit or learning to recognize subtle signs such as changes in body temperature or mucus.

Not every couple can conceive. In fact, one-sixth of all couples that try to get pregnant find that, for one reason or another, they are sterile. The good news for these folks is that times have never been better for using alternative methods of conception. Some of these were mentioned in the previous chapter, along with adoption, as ways of having a baby without having sex. The bad news is that some of these methods are very expensive.

Eventually, however, most couples using some combination of the three strategies above will get the job done without resorting to reproductive technology. But it can take a while. This raises an interesting question: Why is sex so inefficient at making babies? From an evolutionary point of view, even strategy #1—having sex all the time—seems like overkill. Not that I am complaining, mind you. But a woman usually releases only one egg every thirty days. According to one source, that egg is open to fertilization for only six to seventy-two hours, tops. That means that most of the times we make love there is no egg present to be fertilized!

It would be much more efficient to *know* when one is ovulating, to go at it like dogs in heat during that brief period, and not to bother with sex at all during the lengthy infertile period. Which, as we saw in chapter 3, is what many animals do. But for some reason, natural selection has not given us humans any obvious way of knowing when ovulation is happening. This is so strange, that there must be a special reason for it. In biological terms, sex is very expensive. The time that our ancient ancestors spent having sex when reproduction was literally impossible—because there was no egg present—would have been better spent getting food, seeking shelter, and so on. Plus, couples preoccupied with making love would have been vulnerable to predators or enemies. You would think that nature would come up with a better design for passing down copies of our genes.

And actually it has...but only in other animals. For instance, we all know from watching nature documentaries that when certain types of female primates are ovulating, their hinnies light up like neon signs in a red light district, a huge advertisement for any male. These animals' bodies are virtually screaming, "Take me! Take me NOW!" and their behavior sends the same signal. When they are not ovulating, their rumps lack this coloration and their interest in sex fades. Unlike humans, they don't waste time having sex when there is no chance of conceiving.

What's going on here? Why didn't wife go into heat when she was ovulating?

RED RUMPS REVISITED—
WHY WOMEN DON'T HAVE THEM

It looks like natural selection designed ovulation to be hidden. But why would it do that? What possible function could concealed ovulation have served? There are currently two "just-so" theories favored by evolutionary biologists. As it turns out, both of them may be right. Hiding ovulation may have served two different functions at two different times in our evolutionary history. But the story is even more complicated than that. It also turns out that subtle cues for ovulation are available, and that men—at least unconsciously—can detect those cues!

Let's start at the beginning. Very early in the evolutionary story, concealed ovulation evolved as a way that moms could protect their baby from getting killed by adult males who were not the infant's father. Take a moment to reread the last sentence, because it is enough to shock anyone. That's right. *Concealing ovulation helped reduce the risk of infanticide.* Here's how it seems to have happened:

In the beginning, a female's periods of fertility were visible to anyone who cared to notice. Males noticed. This was long before the time when love evolved to bond couples together in pairs. Instead, these very early ancestors mated in a harem system, with a dominant male monopolizing several females. What's more, lovemaking was conducted in full view of others in the group. In this situation, the dominant male could be the only guy to have sex with a female during her brief, well-advertised fertile period. In this way, he could "ensure" (not consciously, of course) that any offspring she bore were his. But since sexual relations occurred in public, other males would "know" (not consciously, of course) that the infant wasn't theirs. And if they ever got the opportunity to impregnate the ape-woman themselves, these other early ape-men would sometimes kill such a child. Why would they do that?

Disturbing as it may be, there is a simple, grim evolutionary logic to this infanticide. A female who is nursing a baby under early ancestral conditions cannot get pregnant because breast-feeding serves as a natural contraceptive. A male who is genetically unrelated to the infant can get his genes passed down by killing the baby, thereby making it possible for the female to get pregnant again, and then fertilizing the mother with his own seed. If you don't believe that this can happen, consider the example of modern day female gorillas. Gorillas mate according to a harem system. And the females typically lose at least one baby in their lifetime to infanticide by some male intruder who manages to force her to follow his reproductive agenda.

In fact, infanticide is surprisingly common among many different animals. But the real clincher is the well-established finding by anthropologists that infanticide is common among humans, too. Of course, we find it horrific. But it is, in fact, universal in traditional hunter-gatherer societies and still occurs in many of them despite the relatively recent imposition of laws to prevent it. This is not speculation. Infanticide *can* happen, and it *has* happened throughout human evolutionary history. What concealed ovulation did was to make it less likely.

The grisly fact of infanticide explains how ovulation first came to be concealed rather than advertised. Infanticide is a real threat to the baby, obviously, but also—in reproductive terms—to the mother. After all, she has already invested 40 weeks of pregnancy plus months or years of care in the baby, and her reproductive window is only open so long. Consequently, natural selection came up with a new way of doing things: It pushed mating from a harem system to a more promiscuous system and, at the same time, hid ovulation from view. If an ape-women copulated with several males during the time at which she was fertile, which was a complete mystery, then none of the males who had copulated with her would harm the child. It could be theirs! And so concealed ovulation first evolved along with a promiscuous lifestyle in our very early ancestors. At the same time, sex became a more private affair, making it that much more difficult to identify a newborn's father.

Now, don't get excited. No one is saying that nowadays, a baby is born and hordes of men stand adoringly around beaming "This kid might be mine! I guess I won't kill it!" That's just how concealed ovulation *first* evolved, several million years ago. Today, the human mating system seems to be more or less monogamous. While plenty of extramarital sex occurs, we know from genetic tests that the vast majority of babies really do belong to the mother's husband. In the meantime, concealed ovulation has taken on a new function.

What happened was this:

After concealed ovulation evolved, some species—chimpanzees are a familiar example—kept a promiscuous mating system. But humans branched off in another direction: monogamy. Now that ovulation was (more or less) hidden, it started to make more sense for an ancestral man and woman to stick together for a while. For one thing, since he didn't know when she was fertile, he would have to stick around to make love with her as often as possible if he was going to succeed in passing his genes down to a future generation. In addition, with the timing of ovulation a complete mystery, sleeping around in the old promiscuous way was no longer worth it. If he left one mate to copulate with a second one, that female may also be ovulating, but she would also probably be in a more or less monogamous relationship with another male. That was the social system in which we evolved. Anyway, if the original mate did leave, then he also opened up the possibility for another guy to come along and hit on his mate at home while she was ovulating! Since there is a significant muscular difference between men and women, a woman would have had little recourse, if a larger male did want to copulate. From the female's point of view, a monogamous mating system meant that she could pick a good ape-man and convince him to stay around and help protect and provide for her and the baby.

Others have argued the existence of concealed ovulation from a female perspective. We must remember that we live in a society of privilege and with access to excellent prenatal care. This is not so for many women around the world today and it was not so for our ancestors. Pregnancy and birth put a female at the greatest risk of death and predation. Therefore, it is possible that concealed ovulation evolved so that women themselves could not actively avoid pregnancy.

And so, as happens with the evolutionary story of many traits, the function of concealed ovulation actually changed over the course of time. The most recent function is the one that most closely fits our intuitions about sexual and marital relations as we experience them today. It is also the most heartwarming one: once it had evolved, concealed ovulation was maintained by natural selection because it promoted a successful strategy of monogamy, private lovemaking, and co-parenting.

So if it takes you a while to conceive, you can blame concealed ovulation. Just remember that concealed ovulation evolved to help keep couples like the two of you together in the first place.

CONCEALED OVULATION ... REVEALED?

While humans do not advertise ovulation with red bumps or mating calls, as some of our primate cousins do, it turns out that ovulation is not as concealed as we once thought. Below, we provide a partial list of some subtle changes that take place over the menstrual cycle.

On high fertility days as compared to low fertility days, women are more likely to accept an offer by a man to dance, more likely to choose outfits that are rated as "sexier" by mixed-sex judges, and more likely to socialize and show increases in locomotor activity (ovulating women get around!).

Physical changes also occur in women during high fertility days. Subtle changes take place in odor, face, body symmetry and voice. These changes occur around the time of ovulation and can be detected by men, who rate ovulating women as more attractive.

And the differences extend beyond physical and behavioral changes. The fertile female also experiences cognitive and perceptual changes that may affect mate choice. Near ovulation, women appear to find male faces with more "masculine" features particularly attractive.

So, is ovulation concealed or not? Evolutionary biologists are still sorting out what these subtle changes really mean. That such changes take place, combined with the uniquely malleable nature of the menstrual cycle, points to a flexibility that may be an evolved response to our social nature. Stay tuned.

A PARTIAL LIST OF SEXY UNIVERSALS

Psychologists have learned a lot about sex. Not surprisingly, given its importance for reproduction, humans are equipped with a vast array of universal behaviors connected with lovemaking. Experts can tell you about the physical features that we respond to, about body language and stages of arousal, and so on. This is a fascinating literature if you can read it without breaking into a sweat and running home to find your mate. But since you are trying to make a baby, running home and making love is probably *exactly* what you should do. So, for your procreative pleasure, here is a very brief overview:

faces. Among other things, a symmetrical face signals good health and is perceived as attractive by both men and women. We all like looking at faces.

breasts. Signal that a female has reached reproductive age. Men everywhere, not just in the West, are interested in breasts.

hips. Men everywhere are also interested in hips, which seem to signal good health and child bearing potential. They rate a female's form as most attractive if her hips are about a third wider than her waist. But any hips will do.

men's body muscle. Tends to impress women by signaling strength.

chest thrust. What men everywhere do to impress a mate. Also used to signal dominance to another male.

courtship feeding. Men around the world offer food or gifts to a woman they are courting.

music. Seems to be a universal or near universal accompaniment to wooing. Along with courtship feeding, this prelude to lovemaking is often neglected by couples desperately trying to conceive after a hard day's work.

smile. A universal facial expression that signals strong interest. Often combined with an eyebrow flash in courting.

eyebrow flash. A 1/6 of a second movement in which the eyebrows are raised and then quickly dropped. Used in all sorts of friendly contacts, including courting.

the coy expression. When a woman cocks her head and looks up shyly at her suitor.

female flirting expression. A smile is followed by an eyebrow raise with the eyes opened wide. This is followed by a dropping of the eyelids, a head tilt down and to the side, and a look away.

the copulatory gaze. When a man or woman stares intently at their mate for 2 to 3 seconds, during which the pupils often dilate. Prevented in some cultures by use of the veil.

pupil dilation. A sign of extreme interest. People judge faces to be more attractive when the pupils are dilated. This effect can be used to one's advantage by turning down the lights or by having a candlelight dinner.

foreplay. Most universal is general body fondling: you know, hugging, patting, stroking…

Phew…is it getting hot in here?
Are you still reading?
Hello?

DR. CRATON'S WARNING: DO NOT USE THIS LAST SECTION TO "GET INTO THE MOOD"

Before we move on to information about pregnancy, there is one final evolutionary insight into sex that I really should share. This is the ultimate answer to the question I know you must be asking yourself as you prepare to make that baby:

Why do we kiss?

Why *do* we kiss? Once you get past the candlelit dinner, mood music, and body language, and you are into the foreplay part of baby-making, you are bound to start kissing. Is kissing universal?

It turns out that your basic, mouth-to-mouth "simple kissing" is *nearly* universal. People kiss in over 90% of the cultures that have been studied. A few cultures seem not to have known about kissing until they discovered it through contact with Western people. Although people in one or two cultures find kissing disgusting, these same people pat, lick, rub, suck, and nip each other as a prelude to intercourse. Tongue kissing is very common across the globe, too, but not universal.

So it looks like kissing is widespread but not built in as an automatic sexual behavior in the same way as, say, a penile erection is. This probably means that it was discovered independently by the various different cultures that practice it. Given the sensitivity of the lips and tongue, which evolved largely to help us eat, it is not surprising that humans in many different cultures hit upon kissing as a pleasurable form of foreplay. But how was it discovered?

One theory is that kissing is derived from "mouth feeding." Ancient hunter-gatherers nursed their young, but also supplemented breast milk with solid foods well before their babies had a full set of teeth. To make solid food edible for a little one, a hunter-gatherer mom chewed up food and then passed it directly from her mouth into her baby's mouth. The survival value of this method of feeding is obvious. It's also not hard to see how mouth feeding without the food—kissing—then became an expression of affection that had its roots as a nurturing, parental behavior. And once this occurred it seems possible that this same expression of affection found its way into the lovemaking repertoire of adults in many societies.

I remember pondering this theory when I first ran across it in a graduate seminar on evolutionary approaches to understanding behavior. "Any comments about the reading?" the professor asked one day at the beginning of class. We had just read a wide-ranging book on the evolutionary origins of many behaviors. "About this idea that kissing came from mouth feeding…" I said, "Isn't that…ahem…a little hard to swallow?"

Sometimes I still think it's a bit hard to swallow. But that's probably because I find it hard to connect the enjoyable act of kissing with a behavior that passes food from one mouth to another! Mouth feeding seems mildly repulsive to us in the modern west (although I do recall sharing gum this way with a girlfriend in high school). No parent I know mouth feeds. Instead, we now have mechanical means of "pre-masticating" our babies' food: blenders puree it for us, or we buy jars of baby food. In addition, we tend to start our kids on solid foods at a later age than our hunter-gatherer ancestors did. But in ancient times mouth feeding would have had obvious survival value. And the chain of reasoning makes sense, even though it's speculative. So I think this mouth feeding theory of the origins of kissing may just be true. Kissing is an odd sort of thing to do—can you think of a better explanation for it? (I'll just let you chew on that one for a while.)

HAPPY PROCREATING TO YOU

Think about it. Humans come in two basic designs: male and female. All the dating, kissing, flirting, and loving that you have ever experienced, all of it, was made possible by the evolution of sex a billion years ago. There is a huge, complex web of universal human behavior and feeling associated with sex and mating. And all of it is, ultimately, about making babies. Which is what you have decided to do.

So have a nice meal, put on some mood music, dim the lights, smile and give your lover your best copulatory gaze. Then let nature take its course.

Chapter 7

EATING WELL DURING PREGNANCY

From an evolutionary point of view, you might wonder, "how much control do I really have over my pregnancy?" Although we noted the many built-in, involuntary aspects of our sexual behavior in the previous chapter, you do have some control over certain aspects of sex: when and with whom, for instance. But now that you've conceived, it seems that Mother Nature is taking over in a big way. Natural selection has designed your body so that it can grow a baby "automatically," without any conscious effort on your part. That tiny, multiplying cluster of cells inside you is developing into a baby at an incredible rate, and your body is not consulting you about any of it!

Here are a few things you can control:

- what you ingest,
- your lifestyle, and
- who provides you with prenatal care.

Control is nice. The challenge is to decide what to do with it. To make good choices about what to put into your body, how to have a healthy lifestyle, and how to get the best possible prenatal care, it helps to understand how natural selection designed pregnancy.

BOTH HARDER AND BETTER

You may already be aware of many of the challenges of parenthood. From our own experiences, we can tell you that it may be harder than you think it's going to be, but also better than you think it's going to be. Even if you already realize it's going to be hard, and even if you already know it's going to be good.

Some parents-to-be are taken by surprise when the hard part starts before the baby is born. Very soon, there may be some serious nausea and other strange discomforts. For example, many foods mom used to enjoy may become inedible. Odors may become stronger and sometimes intolerable. Dad's breath, which was never a sweet perfume, may become thoroughly disgusting. These and other peculiar symptoms are normal. And they are, in fact, quite ancient.

HANNAH THE HUNTER-GATHERER GETS PREGGERS

Before they conceived, Hannah and her hubby Harold ate a wide variety plants and animals. Driven by a craving for sugar, fat, and salt, and by aversions to things that tasted bitter or smelled rancid, they spent their workdays gathering fresh fruits and vegetables and hunting or scavenging wild animals. Since foraging for plant foods, although painstaking, was more consistently successful than hunting, most of Hannah and Harold's diet was in the fruits and veggies food group. But meat was especially prized and enjoyed whenever someone in the group had a successful hunt and offered to share.

During the first trimester of her pregnancy, Hannah's diet changed dramatically. Once a special treat, meat began to smell horrible to her unless the animal was consumed immediately after it was killed. Even then, when it was cooked over an open fire it became distasteful. Most vegetables also became disgusting to her. They tasted especially bitter and sometimes made her sick to her stomach. Perhaps the only food that she could tolerate well during the first thirteen weeks or so was fruits. Because so many of her stock menu items had become unappetizing, Hannah ate less during her first trimester and didn't gain much weight. In fact, she took off some pounds.

All this changed in the second and third trimesters when Hannah's appetite returned. She resumed eating the foods she had preferred prior to becoming pregnant, eating slightly more than she had before conceiving. Hannah's lean, muscular body gained weight slowly and steadily during the last two trimesters. Her foraging trips continued but became gradually shorter in the weeks just prior to giving birth.

REVENGE OF THE VEGETABLES:
WHY PREGNANCY IS SICKENING

You may have recognized Hannah's first trimester symptoms as "morning sickness," which can occur at any time of day and is more appropriately called pregnancy sickness. Pregnancy sickness is best defined as an aversion to certain odors and tastes. It does not necessarily include nausea or vomiting although, as many moms will attest, losing your lunch is not an uncommon experience. Here's the surprising news: pregnancy sickness during the first trimester is universal. It occurs in all cultures and is documented in written records going back to 2000 B.C. Some women don't experience it, or experience less of it. But this is unusual, and these women are at higher risk for having a miscarriage. Pregnancy sickness, it turns out, is part of a normal, healthy pregnancy.

There are two competing explanations for pregnancy sickness. As with any universal trait, it could be *either* an adaptation that somehow helped our ancestors reproduce successfully, *or* a by-product of some other adaptation. This distinction between genuine adaptations and mere by-products will be important for a number of parenting issues, so let's briefly consider a silly example just to be sure it's clear.

Take belly buttons. We all have one, so they are universal. But the belly button itself is not an adaptation. By itself, it didn't promote the survival of our ancient hunter-gatherer ancestors. (At times Linc has wondered whether the function of his "innie" is to collect lint, but that is another story...) But the umbilical cord that once was attached to us *is* an adaptation. It is nature's solution to the problem of how to provide nourishment to us while we're in the womb. The universal navel is just a by-product of this other genuine adaptation, the umbilical cord.

Practically speaking, there is no obvious reason to care whether the belly button is an adaptation or just an evolutionary by-product. But as you'll soon see, determining whether pregnancy sickness is an adaptation has important implications for the health of our children.

Let's start with what happens, hormonally. Very early in pregnancy progestin levels rise dramatically. High progestin levels are necessary to sustain the pregnancy and the developing embryo itself causes the ovary to secrete high levels of this hormone. You may recall that its very name, "progestin" is a contraction of "pro-gestational hormone." Even if an embryo is healthy, some women may miscarry if their ovaries aren't secreting enough progestins early in pregnancy. Fortunately, this can be monitored and addressed by a physician. If there is a problem with the embryo early on, the embryo itself will not induce the changes necessary to cause the ovary to secrete these high levels of progestins, and this may lead to a miscarriage.

In addition to sustaining the pregnancy, progestins change the way the mom feels. As they are metabolized, some of their by-products work at the very same receptors where alcohol works. The result is that they lead women to avoid certain foods by inducing a sense of nausea and light-headedness, just as we experience when we ingest too much alcohol.

Many physicians still believe that a woman's pregnancy sickness, like her belly button, is just an evolutionary by-product. Specifically, they believe that the nausea and aversions that she experiences are just the uncomfortable side effects of the increased levels of hormones in her body that kick in after conception occurs.

These hormonal changes are clearly adaptations; they evolved to sustain pregnancy. But researcher Margie Profet does not think that pregnancy sickness is merely a by-product. She has another hypothesis. In her book, *Pregnancy Sickness: Using Your Body's Natural Defenses to Protect Your Baby-to-Be*, Profet suggests that pregnancy sickness itself is an adaptation; that it evolved because it actually helped our ancient hunter-gatherer ancestors reproduce successfully.

How did it do that?

Brace yourself. You may never look at vegetables the same way again.

Profet presents a compelling argument that "pregnancy sickness protects the embryo from naturally occurring plant toxins in the mother's diet that can cause birth defects or miscarriage. It does this by causing the mother to become repulsed by smells and tastes that indicate toxicity." Naturally occurring toxins? Birth defects? What is she talking about?!

Here's Profet's line of reasoning:

All vegetables contain toxins. Vegetables are plants. Plants, from an evolutionary perspective, survived and reproduced most successfully by evolving ways of protecting themselves from the animals that like to eat them. Since they couldn't run away from these predators, natural selection came up with another kind of defense: chemical warfare. Nature designed plants to make chemicals, called toxins, which exist solely to harm plant-eating animals.

This will seem odd at first. It may make you feel a bit queasy in the supermarket—not to mention your backyard vegetable garden. All those supposedly healthy vegetables are, indeed, loaded with toxins! Was mom wrong when she told us to eat our broccoli?

All people have built-in defenses against these toxins. Of course, mom was right. Vegetables are good for you. Those fresh veggies are loaded with vitamins and nutrients essential to our health. And so animals, not to be outdone in the surviving and reproducing department, have evolved ways of handling plant toxins.

For instance, we have livers and other organs that produce "detoxification enzymes" which break toxins down into harmless substances inside our bodies.

In addition, natural selection gave us the ability to detect these toxins through smell and taste. That's why some things smell rancid or taste bitter. It's our toxin-detector alarm system going off.

And just in case smelling rancidness and tasting bitterness weren't enough, nature added the defenses of nausea and vomiting to help us avoid or expel toxins. That's right, folks. Puking is an adaptation! There's an area of our brain where the blood brain barrier is weaker. This may not seem like a good idea, but it is, because it allows this one area to be affected by toxins. It's called the area postrema, and it is the part of your brain that triggers vomiting. The vomit center, so to speak. So if there are toxins that our brain detects via the area postrema, we have a sense of nausea, which prevents us from ingesting more. Then vomiting allows us to get rid of the toxic substance.

We are also designed to easily remember, dislike and avoid foods that have previously made us sick; psychologists call these learned taste aversions. (At the age of 12, one of us tried drinking two milk glasses filled with undiluted scotch; to this day, the mere sight or smell of the stuff makes me queasy!).

Thus it is that we can eat many toxin-saturated veggies safely and benefit from their nutrients, because our bodies are designed to handle the toxins they contain or to tell us when the toxin levels are dangerously high. All human beings everywhere have these defenses. It's not hard to see why. Early humans who had these traits would have gotten the nutrients, vitamins and minerals they needed without being harmed by naturally occurring toxins. Natural selection would have wasted no time in weeding out any individuals who happened to enjoy the taste of highly toxic foods! Our bodies are designed for selecting healthy foods in a hunter-gatherer environment that contained not only hostile animals, but "hostile" plants as well.

Thanks to Profet and her Darwinian take on food, we now see the produce section in the supermarket as a kind of war zone. Today our veggies are bred to be sweeter tasting so they are less toxic than the bitter stuff Hannah and Harold had to stomach. But those green beans, tomatoes, basil, eggplant, and whatnot still contain toxins that exist for the sole purpose of hurting us! That came as quite a shock.

Some natural toxins in food may cause birth defects. Still, the big shock— just an educated guess, at this point—is that the same amount of toxins that a human adult can tolerate might actually harm a developing embryo. Toxins that cause birth defects when ingested by a pregnant woman are called teratogens. Profet readily admits that there is currently no *direct* evidence that the any of the thousands of toxins present in the plants we eat are teratogens. But, as she points out, this is not because the crucial studies to determine the effects of these naturally occurring toxins on developing human embryos have been conducted. They haven't. Until they have, there is a whole bunch of *indirect* evidence that ought to concern us parents.

For starters, some human foods have been shown to produce birth defects in animals. Why should humans be any different? In addition, pregnancy sickness is most prevalent in the first trimester, when organs and limbs are forming. Is it a coincidence that pregnancy sickness is perfectly timed to discourage moms from ingesting foods containing toxins precisely when these toxins can produce their harmful effects?

Most universals involve variation between individuals, and pregnancy sickness is no exception. For instance, there are individual differences in the severity and duration. This probably has less to do with total increases in hormones and more to do with an individual's sensitivity to those increases, along with her body's ability to adjust to the high levels of hormones. Women who are very sensitive to the surge in hormones will likely experience more severe pregnancy sickness. Similarly, women who can eventually adjust to the increasing hormone levels probably experience an end to pregnancy sickness before those whose bodies' take longer to adjust. Pregnancy sickness can last for one's entire pregnancy, but in most cases it does not. Anecdotally, many women who have been pregnant with both boys and girls will also attest that their pregnancy sickness was worse when they were pregnant with their daughters. So far, data to do not confirm this, but perhaps the right study just hasn't been conducted!

So What?

Why does it matter whether pregnancy sickness is an evolutionary adaptation or just an evolutionary by-product?

You might look at it this way. What if someone were to tell you that they had some advice, based on our present knowledge, that couldn't hurt your baby-to-be but might help her chances of healthy development? You might figure that it's worth following that advice. If we understand that pregnancy sickness may be an adaptation, then we can figure out ways to get adequate nutrition without risk to our babies-to-be.

But even if Profet is right, won't my pregnancy sickness guide me in choosing a good diet for the first trimester? Can't I just listen to my body? This is true to a certain extent, and it was certainly true for Hannah the hunter-gatherer. As a modern-day mom-to-be, however, you face three problems Hannah never confronted.

First of all, the standard dietary advice you are likely to hear from physicians does not distinguish between the first trimester and the rest of pregnancy. We all want healthy babies, and since we've been told all our lives that eating healthy means eating your veggies, we're easily convinced that eating veggies, and lots of them, is the thing to do once you're pregnant. It's only when you look at veggies, eating, and pregnancy from an evolutionary perspective that this advice becomes suspect. Veggies are great both *before* pregnancy and again *after* the first 13 weeks of pregnancy, but we ought to be more critical of the generic dietary advice *during the first trimester* when our babies-to-be are forming their organs and limbs.

A second problem is that unless you are aware that pregnancy sickness may be an adaptation, you may be tempted to manage its symptoms in ways that are potentially harmful. The most dramatic example of this occurred during the late 1950s and 1960s, when many European women took the drug thalidomide to help counter the symptoms of pregnancy sickness. Women who did so during the first trimester had babies with severe birth defects; their limbs were either absent or incompletely developed. Although thalidomide was taken off the market, other well-meaning treatments may be problematic as well. Some "natural family living" books prescribe herbal remedies such as herbal teas to ease your nausea. The mistake here is to assume that "herbal" means "natural" means "good for you and your embryo." Just because something is "natural" or "organic" doesn't mean that it's a good idea to ingest it, especially in large quantities during the first trimester of pregnancy. Herbs have their pungent smells because they contain a ton of toxins. Here is a case where the "natural" cure may be much worse than the problem.

There's a third reason to be fully conscious of the possible function of pregnancy sickness rather than just "listening to your body" as a guide to what is safe to ingest during the first trimester. Being aware in this way helps you recognize potentially harmful situations when pregnancy sickness provides no protection. For instance, unlike Hannah the hunter-gatherer we have modern culinary techniques for masking the bitterness of foods that are high in toxins in order to make them more palatable. We coat them in butter, or sugar, or salt for instance. (As Mary Poppins sings, "a spoonful of sugar helps the medicine go down.") This helps us eat less palatable foods, but it does not remove the toxins from them, of course. In addition, pregnancy sickness does not protect our embryos from modern-day toxins that did not exist during hunter-gatherer times. Evolution has not had nearly enough time to design mothers to avoid alcohol, cigarettes, recreational drugs, medicines, mercury in fish, or junk food. Unfortunately, in this modern world your best bet is to be fully conscious of everything you put into your body.

BUT WILL I GET ADEQUATE NUTRITION?

At this point, you may be wondering whether it's possible to get the nutrition your baby-to-be needs without exposing her to potentially harmful toxins. If you follow Profet's advice during the first trimester and avoid high-toxin veggies, won't you and you're baby-to-be miss out on important nutrients? Several strategies will help ensure that you and your baby-to-be are getting adequate nutrition:

- Even before you become pregnant, take prenatal vitamins
- drink plenty of water—it may make you feel ill, so if you have to mask the taste of water with sugar, then that's what you'll have to do
- let your natural aversions, your knowledge of what foods contain naturally occurring toxins, and your awareness of the potential harmful effects of these foods guide you during the crucial organ formation period of the first trimester
- continue taking prenatal vitamins after you are pregnant— if the gag reflex is too strong, try taking them at night or ask your doctor to prescribe a smaller vitamin

- if taking the iron supplement makes you gag or just creates ridiculously uncomfortable constipation, have a breakfast cereal that provides 100% of the RDA of iron—this way, you'll address both the iron situation and the constipation situation! (A brilliant tip from SRG's ob/gyn—thanks Dr. Sue!).

The best way to ensure that you have adequate stores of vitamins and nutrients is to eat healthy before you become pregnant, and then do your best through the first trimester of pregnancy. Let's look at a Darwinian diet for the special case of healthy eating during the first trimester of pregnancy. Disclaimer: The information below is a distillation of recommendations made by Marjie Profet in her book—we, of course, recommend that you both read her book and consult your physician before modifying your diet dramatically.

A DARWINIAN DIET FOR THE FIRST TRIMESTER

Fresh fruits and pasteurized milk form the foundation of the Darwinian Diet, followed by grains, pastas, and starches. All of these foods are low in naturally occurring toxins. Below, we provide some details.

Eat fresh fruits. You might wonder why fruits are low in toxins, since they come from plants just like their high-toxin vegetable cousins. The answer is that fruits are designed by natural selection to attract animal predators, so they will be eaten and their seeds will be pooped out and grow up into new fruit plants some distance away from the shade of the parent. That's why fruit tastes sweet instead of bitter! The exception of course is the outer skin or peel, which is high in toxins to keep insects from devouring the fruit before the seeds are mature. Thus banana peels taste very bitter. (It goes without saying that you don't want to eat any banana peels during the first trimester!).

Fruits are a great food choice whether you are pregnant or not, since they are loaded with vitamins. So start your first trimester diet with lots of fruit, and eat as much of it as you want. There were no pesticides in Hannah the hunter-gatherer's day, but there are now—these are undetectable by your nose and taste buds. Because pesticides are applied to the outside avoid the peels, wash the fruit thoroughly and then peel it.

Eat grains. As far as grain-based starchy foods go, you may find that processed grains like plain white bread are more palatable than whole grain products. This is because processing removes the outer husks of the grains, where most of the natural toxins are located. In one sense, modern moms-to-be are fortunate compared to Hannah the hunter-gatherer. In good times Hannah could find fruits to help her through the first trimester, but anthropologists tell us she didn't have *any* foods in the grains or dairy groups available to her. No wonder she lost weight until the second trimester! Because a modern day mom-to-be has many more palatable and non-toxic foods to choose from, she can expect to gain two or three pounds during the first trimester. But she shouldn't worry if her pregnancy sickness leads her to lose a couple pounds. Continue to check with your doctor, though, if losing more than a few pounds or if symptoms of dehydration appear.

Be careful with vegetables. Vegetables are nature's vitamin-rich toxin producers (or is it toxin-rich vitamin producers?). According to Profet, based on what we currently know, the smartest strategy for veggies is to eat small quantities of the least bitter ones (such as green beans, carrots, tomatoes, peas) and simply avoid the particularly bitter ones (broccoli, Brussels sprouts, peppers). A second tip is to avoid eating the same vegetables all the time. Humans—like rats and unlike koala bears (who only need eucalyptus leaves to stay healthy)—are omnivores. That is, we are designed to eat many different foods rather than focusing on a single food. You've probably heard that eating a wide variety of foods is a good idea, since each food only provides a portion of the many nutrients your body needs. The same sort of reasoning applies when we are trying to avoid high doses of any particular natural toxin. Since different vegetables typically contain different toxins, you will limit your embryo's exposure to any one toxin by eating a range of items (but only the less bitter ones). So, as Profet puts it, "diversify your toxins"! You may be doing your baby-to-be an enormous favor.

Finally, unwashed fruits and vegetables that grow in or near the ground may contain the harmful *toxoplasmosis* bacteria. Wash everything first.

Be careful with meat. Plants aren't the only source of natural toxins in a modern diet. Meat attracts bacteria (toxoplasmosis, coliform and salmonella, for example) that produce toxins. In fact, several researchers who have followed up on Profet's work believe that the reason pregnancy sickness evolved is to protect the baby-to-be from meat-borne pathogens, rather than naturally occurring toxins in plants. It's suggested that pregnant women do not eat any raw meat. This includes avoiding obvious dishes like medium rare filet mignon or cheeseburgers, but it also includes avoiding less obvious things like sushi. Barbequed and smoked foods are also to be avoided because of the toxins that result with those kinds of preparations. So, for example, lox are off the table. Deli meats also are not an option—these may harbor the harmful bacteria, *listeria*.

Be careful with modern foods that contain "natural" ingredients. Other foods we should be wary of include a variety of modern culinary inventions that incorporate natural ingredients that may contain toxins. Examples include beverages derived from bitter plant parts (coffee, tea, herb teas and colas), all spices and herbs used for flavoring, and other bitter plants used for flavorings such as onions, garlic, hot peppers, and mustard. The extreme pungency or bitterness of these items is an indication of the enormous amount of toxins they contain. According to Profet, during the first trimester, these items are best considered guilty until proven innocent. Your body may do this for you, automatically, but if it doesn't now you know. If possible try to avoid caffeine during the first trimester—cutting out caffeine all at once may induce unbearable headaches for which you cannot take any medicine, so ideally you might start the process before you are pregnant. Remember not to fool your toxin-detectors by hiding the bitterness of these items behind a layer of sugar or salt—the toxins are still in there.

Soft cheeses like Brie, camembert, and feta are best avoided; these may contain *listeria*. For the same reason, avoid things like fresh squeezed fruit juice and sprouts like alfalfa and radishes. Keep in mind that in the first trimester, fresh is not always best. Some kinds of freshly made foods, like Caesar salad dressing or homemade ice cream, often contain raw eggs. These may contain salmonella—it's best to avoid them altogether.

The Darwinian diet as summarized above is obviously not an exhaustive list of foods to select or to avoid, but it does provide a general framework for you. There are plenty of websites that contain very useful information on the topic and your healthcare provider should also supply you with such a list that might contain foods that are more prevalent in your area.

If you are skeptical about the above dietary advice, believe us when we say that we are sympathetic. It would be a lot easier to jump into a Darwinian diet if we had direct evidence that specific foods cause birth defects. But the fact is that the necessary studies have not been conducted. We should be watching to see what evidence is gathered in the next decade or so. The sort of research that is required is hard to conduct, since it is most likely needs to be "retrospective," relying on self-reported memories about what subjects ate many weeks earlier. People are not very good at recalling this kind of information over such a long time period. In addition, whether birth defects occur and what type of birth defects occur will depend not only on what food was eaten but at what point in prenatal development exposure occurred. Sorting out causes and effects will be a major challenge. Stay tuned.

In the meantime, we hope that thinking about pregnancy sickness as nature's way of protecting your child from harm brings you some peace of mind. You'll be horrified to learn that in the recent past, psychologists—followers of Freud, in particular—blamed women for their pregnancy sickness! In some cases, women were told that nausea and vomiting reflected their neurotic ambivalence about motherhood, and that they were symbolically trying to "expel" their baby from their body. One harsh therapy even had women isolated in hospital beds, lying in their own vomit! An evolutionary perspective, on the other hand, can provide comfort and serenity. It says: if you can't feel good, you can at least feel good about your nausea's function!

Now that we've discussed *what* to eat, we turn to the question of *how much* to eat.

Chapter 8

HOW MUCH WEIGHT SHOULD I GAIN?

...all the right junk in all the right places
-Meghan Trainor

Weight is an enormous issue in our culture today, and the controversies and conflicting advice only intensify when you become pregnant. Women express two principal concerns about weight gain during pregnancy. The first is that they want to do what's healthiest for their baby-to-be and for themselves. The second concern is considered more controversial because it is "merely aesthetic": many women worry that pregnancy will ruin their girlish figures forever. Often they hint at both of these concerns, for example by asking what is the least amount of weight they can gain while still having a healthy pregnancy.

Others, however, see the mere suggestion that women control their weight gain during pregnancy as an obnoxious male-chauvinist-pig plot. According to some (but by no means all) sources, women who aspire to recover their pre-pregnancy bodies as soon as possible after giving birth are buying into our male-dominated culture's obsession with thinness. Since the medical profession is just as male-dominated as the rest of the culture, these sources argue, any medical advice about weight control is ultimately really just an expression of men's culturally-based taste for thin women.

As it turns out, an evolutionary approach to the question of optimal weight gain during pregnancy points to a solution that is both healthy and attractive.

BEFORE PREGNANCY: REPRODUCTIVE FAT VERSUS FAT FAT

One exquisite design feature of the female body is that it won't allow you to reproduce if you are not getting enough to eat. To grow, breastfeed, and care for a baby, a hunter-gatherer mom-to-be needed a reliable energy supply. This energy came from food, either directly soon after she ate or indirectly from the stored fat created when the calories she consumed exceeded her immediate energy requirements. That's what fat is: a reserve supply of energy.

Following nature's design, you started adding fat to your lower body soon after puberty. While the boys in school were gaining muscle mass, you were gaining hips, a butt and thighs. This is good, healthy, reproductive fat. It's there to support the energy requirements of motherhood. Thus, "fat," is not a four letter word—although, we often treat it this way. Our bodies need fat. Fat is important for pregnancy and nursing because the calories provided by fat sustain the additional energy demands required during those two critical times. More than that, the developing baby particularly needs fats to produce the specialized cells and connections within their brains. Lipids—constituents of fats—are critical for proper brain development. This is true beginning in the second trimester and continues until the baby is at least two years old. This is one reason that whole milk is recommended by pediatricians after weaning and until age two. Fat is critically important.

Amazingly, your body is able to keep track of how much of it you have. It only ovulates normally if you have a certain amount of reproductive fat and have maintained a stable weight for a while. This is a wonderful adaptation, when you consider that malnourishment from starvation was a common experience for our hunter-gatherer ancestors. When food was scarce and mom herself was not getting enough nutrition, a baby's chances of making it were slim indeed. Women who conceived only when food was sufficiently plentiful had a distinct reproductive advantage over those whose bodies did not have this sensitivity to environmental conditions.

Thankfully, starvation due to an actual shortage of food is much less common in modern industrial society. However, an alarming number of modern day women are fooling their bodies into "famine mode" through excessive dieting. The same mechanism that inhibits ovulation in a starving hunter-gatherer is activated when a woman suffers the self-starvation of anorexia or bulimia. These women frequently become so underweight that they start having irregular periods and, often, stop having their periods altogether (called amenorrhea). Similarly, female athletes who diet and train intensely such as runners, swimmers, and ballet dancers, and other women who significantly lower their body fat, such as models, have a high incidence of delayed menarche, irregular cycles and amenorrhea.

Don't assume that as long as you get enough calories to become pregnant you are eating healthy. That was true for hunter-gatherer moms-to-be like Hannah, but is not nearly as likely to be true for us. Like you, Hannah couldn't get pregnant unless she had maintained a certain caloric intake and had the body fat to show for it. But her situation was quite different from yours. *All she ate were fruits, vegetables, and lean meats.* As long as she consumed enough food, she automatically had enough vitamins and nutrients stored to support the early development of her baby-to-be.

Because our modern diets include many foods that are calorie-rich but nutrient-poor, a modern day woman can become pregnant without having an impressive store of nutrients to support her early pregnancy. The stone-age mechanism that determines whether a woman is well nourished enough to handle motherhood is fooled by the presence of fat into assuming that she has plenty of nutrition as well. That was always true in hunter-gatherer times, but it *may not* be true for you! The only way to know for sure is to pay attention to what goes into your mouth in the weeks before you conceive. Serious vitamin deficiencies are rare, but mild ones are common. This is why it is recommended that women who plan to conceive begin taking prenatal vitamins, even before they become pregnant.

The difference between healthy reproductive fat and unhealthy high risk fat is not simply a matter of how much a woman has, although that is important. Where the fat is located on her body is crucial. Good fat is in the lower body, and gives a healthy woman the classic female pear shape. Researchers refer to this as a "gynoid" distribution of body fat. Unhealthy fat is put on in the belly, giving a woman an apple shape that researchers call "android" (really! we're not joking, that's what they call it). The gynoid/android distinction is a matter of the *ratio* of the amount of abdominal fat to the amount of lower body fat.

Today, cultures around the world vary in *how much* fat they consider to be attractive; our Western thinness fetish is apparently not shared by all our fellow species members. What is universal, however, is that people everywhere rate the gynoid shape as more attractive than the android shape. Since a gynoid shape is a good indicator of health and thus fertility, it is not surprising that evolution built men to prefer pear-women to apple-women. Consider.

- You first became gynoid when you hit sexually maturity.
- You become less gynoid and more android at menopause.
- The only other time you are designed by nature to become android is when you're pregnant.
- Even anorexic women who have stopped menstruating are gynoid; in fact they are hyper-gynoid, with an unusually high ratio of lower body fat to upper body fat despite their very low total body fat.

Being gynoid is apparently an advertisement that a woman is fertile. Even the case of anorexic women makes a lot of evolutionary sense, if you think about it. Because our ancestors frequently dealt with short-term food shortages they would have alternated between periods of fertility and infertility. It would pay for a woman to keep "advertising" her reproductive potential by retaining a gynoid shape even if she lost weight and became temporarily infertile during one of those brief food shortages.

Excessive weight gain before, during, or after pregnancy was simply never a problem for our ancient hunter-gatherer ancestors. In fact, as we've seen, they had the opposite problem. These early women—our great, great, great (and so on) grandmothers—had to cope with frequent food shortages and the constant threat of starvation. As a result, natural selection designed women's bodies to "know" whether they have enough fat to support a baby.

Until we stopped being hunter-gatherers a mere 10,000 years ago—just yesterday in evolutionary terms—*nature had no experience with overweight people*. There are no evolved mechanisms to prevent us from overindulging in the many tasty high calorie foods available in the modern world, even though doing so can ultimately make us very sick. On the contrary, nature has built each of us to crave sweet and fatty foods, since in ancient natural environments such cravings ensured that we sought out sufficient calories. So in this high calorie modern world it is exceedingly easy to become plump, or worse.

And plump we are. In the U.S., the situation is particularly grim. By some measures, more than half the women are overweight and the percentage of overweight adults is increasing every year. The new seats that are being installed in stadiums and on public transportation have become wider, to accommodate our expanding collective behind.

Judgmental remarks about being overweight may shock or offend you. Don't heavy people already experience enough "size prejudice"? Still worse, doesn't this attitude just encourage unhealthy starvation dieting and dysfunctional eating habits? These are important and complex questions. In terms of health, though, the answers are clear.

The research shows, unequivocally, that the risk of health problems increases the more overweight one becomes. For starters, being overweight means being at higher risk for diabetes; infants of diabetic women have a threefold increase in the risk of serious birth defects. Being overweight also substantially increases your risk of heart disease, including coronary artery disease, high blood pressure, and stroke. You also have an increased risk of developing cancer of the breast, colon and uterus, and your risk of developing gallstones increases. Pregnant women who are very obese, even if they are not diabetic, are more likely than lighter women to deliver an infant with spina bifida or other major birth defects. And pregnant women who are obese also have a greater-than-normal chance of getting gestational diabetes, toxemia, and blood clots in the legs.

Because even small weight losses produce measurable health benefits, every pound counts when you're overweight. But the weeks immediately before pregnancy are not the time to go on a "diet," if by that you mean trying out one or more of the many gimmicks, plans and programs sold to us by the weight loss industry. Actually, we know that these programs don't work in the long run. And at any rate, you don't want to be restricting your intake of nutrients at this time; you want to be storing them up! Whatever your current state of health is, you can begin the lifelong process of becoming healthier by starting a simple three-step plan.

- Follow the Darwinian diet for the first trimester of pregnancy.
- Limit, but do not eliminate, carbohydrates.
- Become more active.

It may seem oversimplified, but the above three steps are the key for all of us, pregnant or not. So perhaps we should take a break right now, eat a piece of fruit, and then take a walk. When we get back, we'll look at where the weight gain recommendations for pregnancy come from.

How Much to Expand When You're Expecting

The First Trimester

You may be surprised to learn that our hunter-gatherer ancestors actually lost weight during the first trimester. But that's because we're not used to treating the vital organ-forming first semester as significantly different from the rest of pregnancy. As we've seen in discussing pregnancy sickness, a woman's body is designed to become very selective about food during this early period of prenatal development. This is a good thing, though it may not feel like it—a mechanism designed by natural selection to protect your baby from harmful toxins. So if your pregnancy sickness leads you to lose a couple of pounds during the first trimester, you shouldn't worry. This happens to many women and it's completely normal.

Here's the rub. Many of us who try to maintain a healthy weight when we aren't pregnant become adept at reasonably restricting our food intake, selecting healthy foods, and drinking lots of water. But now that we are pregnant, those salads and water now make us sick. Diet sodas are off the table because of toxic artificial sweeteners. Many kinds of fish are off the table, too, because of mercury content. And so on. In other words, the healthy stuff that we are accustomed to is either too gross or unsafe. So what the heck is left to eat? Carbs, starchy carbs, and sugary fruit juices. For some of us, that's all we can stomach while in the throes of (all-day) morning sickness. That's why it is really hard not to gain a lot of weight during pregnancy.

One bit of emerging data that may provide some relief is to eat proteins to minimize pregnancy sickness symptoms. Keeping something like a granola bar with protein on your bedside table, so that you can eat it first thing in the morning may help—or not.

The Second and Third Trimesters

As your body adjusts to the higher levels of progestins that cause pregnancy sickness, you may feel like resuming a "normal" diet. Once the second trimester kicks in and (we hope, for your sake) pregnancy sickness fades, your baby-to-be's basic physiological structures are in place. The risk of serious malformation or birth defects is lessening. From here on, it's more about developing those tissues and systems—your teeny-weeny three ounce baby-to-be needs to transform into a seven pound newborn. As if to give you the green light for resuming a normal diet, your body "turns on" your old appetite and food preferences.

Keep your head. Don't interpret the phrase "now you're eating for two" as "now you need to eat as much as two adults"! Doctors currently recommend that a woman of average weight gain between 25 and 35 pounds during pregnancy. In our home state of Massachusetts—where there seems to be a coffee shop on every street corner—only 63 percent currently gain this amount. Twenty-four percent gain between 35 and 49 pounds, and 6.5 percent gain 50 pounds or more!

Don't panic. Sometimes, that weight can be excessive swelling and some women "sweat out" the excessive water after the baby is born. As long as you are having a healthy, typical pregnancy, you want to eat smart and think about how what you put into your body affects your developing baby. Obviously, you don't want to go on a diet while you're pregnant. You run a double risk if you severely restrict your calories during the second or third trimesters. First, you increase the likelihood of having a miscarriage. You do not want your body to think that there is a famine! Just as ovulation is inhibited in extremely underweight women, your body may decide to miscarry if you start losing too much weight. Second, if you don't eat enough you increase the likelihood of having a low birth weight child. You want to be sure that your child gets sufficient calories and essential nutrients—depriving her of these is very dangerous.

All of this affects your baby's life beyond the womb. Scientists have been exploring a hypothesis called the "thrifty metabolism." Essentially, it states that *the in utero* environment sets up metabolic systems for the baby. Particularly if there is a shift from little food to lots of food or from lots of food to not so much, the baby develops a metabolism that is primed for the development of diabetes and cardiovascular disease. And this effect may be taking place even a generation back so that the food availability of your parents will affect the metabolism of your offspring. That will be compounded by a shift in your own food intake. However, some studies show that good early post-natal nutrition might be able to attenuate the effect.

The problem is straightforward: you must eat enough, but not too much. *You need to add about 300 calories a day to your usual intake to support the growth of your baby.* This may not seem like a lot of extra calories, but it is more than adequate for your baby-to-be. It's important, too, that these calories aren't just empty calories, i.e. with little nutritional value.

How much weight should you expect to gain if you follow this plan? Assuming there's only one baby in there, a challenging goal is to try to gain about 25 pounds by the end of your pregnancy. Don't obsess over this number, however.

The following table breaks this weight gain down, part by part:

New Growth	Weight (lbs.)
One baby	7.5
Placenta	2-3
Amniotic fluid	2
Extra uterine tissue	2-5
Breasts	2-3
Extra blood and body fluid	6.5
Fat deposits on butt, thighs, and belly	5-9

Weight recommendations differ depending on a woman's weight at conception. For women whose pre-pregnancy weight is in the normal range, the recommended weight gain is 25-35 pounds. The same source recommends that lean women gain 28-40 pounds, overweight women 15-25 pounds, and obese women at least 15 pounds.

On the other hand, 25 pounds is on the high side when compared to the weight gain shown by modern day hunter-gatherer women bearing healthy babies, which appears to be in the 14-20 pound range. Why are some recommendations for women in industrial societies so much higher than the "natural" weight gain shown by hunter-gatherers? One reason is that public health officials have identified low birth weight—defined as less than 5 pounds 8 ounces—as a public health issue. When addressing such an issue, researchers rely on averages across many different individuals. We know that when moms gain more weight babies do, too. So from a public health perspective it makes sense to try to reduce the incidence of low birth weight by a general recommendation that all moms gain a lot of weight during pregnancy.

However, the recommendation is highly misleading. A healthy, normal-weight mom who does not smoke and is not under a lot of stress is not any more likely to have a low birth weight baby if she gains 20 pounds than if she gains 30. That's because she's unlikely to have a low birth weight baby, period—as far as we can tell, she is simply not at risk. Researchers have yet to sort out all the factors that influence low birth weight. For instance, we don't know if the 14-20 pound gains shown by lean, hard-working hunter-gatherer women are optimal or just adequate. But we do know that they generally deliver healthy babies of normal weight.

Chapter 9

ESTABLISHING A HEALTHY LIFESTYLE

There's nothing like a huge life change—say, imminent parenthood—to make you think about your daily habits of living. Are you getting exercise? How much stress do you experience during a typical day? What do you do for fun and relaxation? Do you ever *have* any fun or relaxation? Reflecting on these questions can lead you to make adjustments that improve how you feel each day. Making these adjustments now will help you handle some of the parenting challenges that lie ahead. And it is not too soon to begin thinking about one of those challenges: providing a positive, healthy model for your child.

But what are healthy habits of living? How can we know for sure what's good for us?

By looking at the "lifestyles" of our ancient hunter-gatherer ancestors, the evolutionary approach helps us get a sense of what levels of physical activity, stress, and leisure our bodies and minds expect. We can then decide whether we want to use this information to find a more balanced way of living, during pregnancy and for the rest of our lives. As we'll see, many mismatches between modern living and our ancient design make healthy living a challenge for modern day parents.

Happily, modern living also affords an enormous range of choices for healthy living, choices that Hannah and Harold could never have imagined. It is up to each of us to improvise a lifestyle from this web of modern obstacles and opportunities—a lifestyle that is particularly tailored to our own needs and goals.

EXERCISE: OR, HOW GROCERY SHOPPING EXPLAINS THE NEED FOR TREADMILLS

Did you ever think that treadmills are stupid? That they are only for fitness nuts or people who had lots of time on their hands?

Maybe you still think treadmills are stupid. Or maybe, like an increasing number of people, you use one three or four times a week or have a gym membership. Our ancient friends Hannah and Harold never used a treadmill. Yet they were lean and muscular. Being physically fit followed inevitably from their lifestyle. Consider the mismatch here:

- Hunting and gathering food requires an extended period of moderate physical activity and burns a lot of calories
- going to the grocery store, on the other hand, just burns gas in our cars.

The next time you're at your local Shop 'Til You Drop, go to the packaged meat section and take a moment to reflect on what a grocery store really is. Those are chunks of flesh in front of you! Animal parts. You have been spared the physical effort involved in tracking and killing a wild animal. As you stand by the produce section, you can have a similar realization: the food industry has done all your foraging for you!

And so, you see, the fact of grocery shopping explains why we need treadmills—or at least *some* modern day substitute for the long foraging hikes of our ancient ancestors. Without some exercise we become sedentary softies. Of course, you can choose to be soft. But if you do you must expect to tire more easily, experience the activities of daily living as more arduous, and become prone to a variety aches and pains. Sometimes those aches, like a backache, can develop into a serious long-term problem. Exercise will also help keep your weight down and is a good thing in general, because it protects us from a variety of truly serious health problems.

Maybe you're convinced already that exercise is a good thing. You nevertheless may wonder whether and how much to exercise while you are carrying your baby-to-be.

EXERCISE DURING PREGNANCY:
THE HUNTER-GATHERER MODEL

Exercise has two enormous benefits. Very early in your pregnancy it may help you sleep better. Unfortunately, this effect may be short-lived. As your pregnancy progresses, sleeping becomes more difficult and some women even experience pregnancy insomnia. Secondly, exercise combats stress. Ask any steady exerciser and they will tell you that it not only makes them stronger, but elevates their mood as well. They have more, not less, energy to put into their daily activities. At the same time, they feel more relaxed and less stressed. This is because exercising releases all kinds of hormones that make us feel happier. There is probably also a psychological benefit to being unplugged from our hectic lives for a short time. When your body does what it was designed to do you become stronger, and you avoid becoming riddled with aches and pains. You are bound to feel more content.

Hannah almost certainly kept going on gathering excursions right up until she gave birth. However, the distances she traveled and the time she spent away from camp probably declined toward the end of her pregnancy. At that point, it's likely that she became somewhat more dependent on others in her social group, those related individuals and her husband who had a stake in the health of the baby. Biology fostered that and it probably also fostered a concern for Hannah's health that stemmed from true affection for her.

Doctors used to advise pregnant women to avoid exercise. No more! So even if you are not a lean, mean hunter-gatherer machine right now you can still find time for pleasurable activities that increase your strength and stamina. You may look at it this way: you are training for the big event of motherhood.

Don't train too hard. Motherhood is not the Olympics. But if you live in an area where health clubs offer "low impact" exercise classes geared specifically to pregnant women, you might want to look into that. If you're doing other forms of exercise, as your pregnancy progresses you'll probably be advised to limit yourself to safe, non-jarring forms of exercise. Late pregnancy is not the time to take up skiing, hang gliding, or skateboarding!

The risk, of course, is that a bad bump or fall could cause you to injure yourself or to miscarry. The latter possibility was sadly driven home to us last year when we walked into an office at work and found a secretary in tears. Her daughter-in-law had just miscarried her firstborn-to-be after getting in a snowmobile collision. So be careful. Sometimes athletes are advised that they can continue training at the same level. Anecdotally, we know of several cases like this and all but one resulted in several complications. So, exercise, but use your own common sense, too.

Even for less exotic and relatively safe forms of exercise you'll eventually need to modify the activity to accommodate your pregnant state. For instance, because lying down puts the weight of the uterus on the vena cava, the vein that carries blood to the heart, it restricts the amount of oxygen that gets to your baby. So you shouldn't exercise or sleep on your back.

When considering what's safe and what's risky, remember that Hannah the hunter-gatherer stayed nice and fit just by walking. During pregnancy, mild forms of exercise like walking are ideal and don't risk harm to your baby-to-be. So grab a good pair of walking shoes with lots of extra support—your body is designed for walking on ground, not pounding on pavement, after all—and start moving! Be prepared to tire easily, though, and let your own fatigue and discomfort lead you to shorten those walks as your due date approaches. And don't be surprised if you hurry to the bathroom more and more!

By the way, if you live in an area where the weather doesn't allow for outdoor walks, you can look up the hours for indoor malls. In many cases the mall itself, but not the stores, will open early specifically for pedestrians. It's free and there are fewer folks around during off hours, so you'll have less exposure to nasty winter illnesses.

As you walk, think about the next fitness activity that parenthood will afford you: the chance to carry your child. If you are a little more fit, then you will be able to carry your baby a lot more. That is not only convenient, but it will help both you and your child through the early months and beyond. If you are reading this in preparation for your second child, and maybe you also have a full-time job outside the home, we realize that you have no time to exercise. Walking may be especially helpful for you.

There are lots of simple things you can do to become just a bit more fit. One suggestion we like is to stop trying to get a "good" parking spot at the grocery store. Walking an extra 50 yards is something. It's not a foraging trip, but that's okay because you've probably never been on a foraging trip before. You should not start while pregnant!

WHY HUNTER-GATHERERS DON'T GET ULCERS

These days we may need sleep-enhancing, stress-reducing exercise more than our hunter-gatherers ever did. That's because we face a constant daily stream of mildly stressful, evolutionarily novel stimuli. Take the case of grocery shopping. We've already noted how convenient it is compared to hunting and gathering. Surprisingly, it is also more stressful!

You may never crumple up and collapse on the floor of aisle seven, but shopping has many of the mild persistent stressors that we must contend with in modern day life: traffic, finding a parking place, crowds of people whom we don't know and with whom we avoid eye contact, strangers we must interact with at the check-out counter, and often some nagging pressure to finish the task of shopping in a reasonable amount of time so we can move on to the next activity in our day. Some studies have even shown that having more options for shopping items like laundry detergent makes us more anxious, not less!

It may seem contradictory that getting our food is both easier and more stressful than was the case for our ancient ancestors, but it's true. Hannah's foraging trips were essentially long but leisurely "power walks," taken two or three days a week depending on the available food supply. Several others, usually women and children, joined her. Filling a sac with a variety of foods and keeping an eye out for freshly dead animals that could be scavenged, she frequently traveled several miles before returning "home" to camp by mid-to-late afternoon. She then helped to distribute and prepare the food, watched the kids, and chatted with the other members of her group. Never once did Hannah come home so fried from her day that she was compelled to make a bubble-bath and exclaim, "Calgon, take me away!"

How does this compare to your life? For many of us, this sounds both physically more demanding and significantly less stressful. We work at physically *un*demanding jobs that provide us with the money to "hunt and gather" food at the grocery store. Whereas Hannah had long periods of continuous exercise as an intrinsic part of her food gathering, it's a challenge to fit exercise into a somewhat chaotic work week.

Note, too, that Hannah had people. She foraged with people she trusted and loved and then came home to a whole extended family of folks who cooperated and socialized with each other. When you come home from work, if you have people, they are probably your husband or your children. You and your husband are probably tired and focused on taking care of the kids. There may be very little time for leisurely chatting and there's probably even less for connecting with other friends or family during a typical work week.

To understand the importance of socializing as not merely pleasurable, but necessary for humans, think of this. Short of a death penalty, what is the worst punishment we can afford an individual? What is the worst thing we can do to someone who is already in jail? Many people would say social isolation. That is the worse punishment we can give someone—even a criminal who is already being punished with a jail sentence.

Without exercise and without social contact, stress becomes exacerbated. But why is stress a problem anyway? Isn't stress "natural"? Indeed it is. Short-term, or acute, stress is natural and even healthy when it motivates us to behave in advantageous ways. Like when a hunter-gatherer runs away from a hungry leopard. Or when we make a last, big push to meet a deadline at work.

But the relentless, chronic stress of modern living is a serious health issue. Among other things, we get ulcers from it. There's a terrific book by Robert Sapolsky entitled *Why Zebras Don't Get Ulcers* that first described and explained this mismatch between modern life and the evolutionary biology we inherited.

Hunter-gatherers don't get ulcers because they didn't experience as much long-term stress as we do.

GOOD STRESS, BAD STRESS

Stressors are things that cause our bodies to get "pumped up" or aroused physiologically. We are all built to experience this universal stress reaction when the situation demands it. Say you are walking in a dark alley at night and you hear footsteps behind you. You experience the classic stress response: your pulse and breathing quicken, your palms get sweaty, and your pupils dilate. Stress hormones begin to flood into your bloodstream.

This universal "fight or flight" response is a wonderful adaptation. It prepared Hannah to respond to the kinds of danger that would have been present in her environment, such as a predator looking for lunch. It evolved because individuals who were physiologically aroused in response to such an immediate threat had better survival rates than those who lacked the stress response.

But danger from a predator—or from menacing footsteps in a dark alley, for that matter—lasts only seconds or minutes. Either you are killed or you get away. If you survive unscathed, your nervous system goes through a universal "winding down" response. Clearly the stress mechanism built into us is designed for brief, highly stressful events. For Hannah the hunter-gatherer, only very extreme conditions such as a serious food shortage or the loss of a mate would have led to a sustained stress response.

When stress is prolonged, we can suffer many ill effects. The research on this is clear: persistent stress makes us prone to illness, darkens our mood, and makes us feel exhausted, burnt out, and overwhelmed. Duh. But here's something that may shock you: if the stress is high enough and prolonged enough, regions of our brains can even shrink in size!

One remarkable line of research provides a nice example of the everyday decrease in quality of life that stress can cause. Researchers recruited subjects to live for several days in a dormitory setting, isolated from social contact from each other—from anyone, in fact, except the researchers themselves. On the first day, subjects completed a stress survey. They then were exposed to the germs that cause the common cold—researchers actually inserted these microbugs into the subjects' noses with droppers! The results probably won't surprise you: subjects who had reported undergoing a lot of stress in their lives were the ones that got sick. When we're burnt out, we get sick more easily.

Short term stress can decrease our risk for illness. Take the example of college students who get sick as soon as they come home from college, after finals. During finals, high levels of stress hormones helped stave off illness, while they ate terribly, slept little and were exposed to all kind of germs studying in close contact with other stressed students. In this case, they don't get sick until the acute, immediate stressor (finals) is removed.

Chronic stress is different. We all know folks who are chronically stressed and often sick. If you experience chronic stress—stress that doesn't let up, unlike the final exam stress—then you are likely to get sick more often and stay sick longer because certain aspects of your immune system are chronically dampened down.

A LITTLE BIT ABOUT THE BIOLOGY OF STRESS

When we use the term stress, we all generally understand its meaning. The "stress response," on the other hand, is our body's reaction to stress. As Sapolsky points out, in the ancient past, humans experienced both acute stress and sometimes more prolonged physical stress from lack of food. Those are the kinds of stressors our bodies can deal with very well. In the first case, we experience the "fight or flight" response. In the second, our bodies have developed numerous mechanisms for dealing with famine, which we have alluded to in chapters 6 and 7.

So let's discuss the biology of fight or flight. When we experience an acute stressor, our body releases several hormones. The first is Corticotropin-releasing hormone or CRH. CRH has effects on its own, but it also elicits the release of another hormone called, adrenocorticotropin hormone or ACTH.

ACTH travels through our body to our adrenal glands where it elicits the release of cortisol, our stress hormone. In addition, our nerves send out lots of epinephrine, or adrenalin. As the phrase "fight or flight" implies, the combined action of all of these molecules is to "get us the heck out of Dodge." Our heart races and our breathing rate increases all in an effort to get oxygen to our voluntary muscles to make an energy molecule that will help us RUN.

We don't just need oxygen, however. We need sugar to make this energy molecule, called ATP. So when we are under stress, CRH aids in getting sugars out of other cells and into our muscles. Now with oxygen and sugars, our muscle cells can make ATP and RUN!

Once we have outrun our opponent, we will begin to feel safe. At this point, we have a bunch of cortisol in our blood. Well, now we need to replenish all the sugar we used up while we were running. The cortisol pushes us to seek out and eat high fat, high carbohydrate food to replenish our calorie stores.

This is our stress response and the recovery from the stress response. It's the one we've inherited, even though we don't usually run away from our bosses at high speed. This is what happens to our bodies, when we ANTICIPATE an unpleasant evening. This is the same thing that happens when we are tired but we still have to make a deadline. This is Sapolsky's argument: same stress response, different life. We may not release these hormones at their highest levels, but they are being released relatively more often that in our ancient past.

In terms of reproductive biology, CRH and cortisol can inhibit every single aspect of the reproductive axis we discussed earlier. CRH and GnRH are even produced by the same tiny structure in the brain, the hypothalamus. Cortisol and CRH can either directly or indirectly inhibit all those hormones that are necessary for our menstrual cycle, as we discussed back in chapter 3: GnRH, LH and FSH and progestins and estrogens. From an evolutionary perspective, this makes sense. Why would you want to get pregnant when you are in acute stress or when there's no food? In our ancient past, if it had been regularly possible for women to get pregnant under these circumstances, they would have either lost the baby during pregnancy or the baby wouldn't have survived long after birth.

STRESS AND PREGNANCY

We all experience some stress in our modern lives—it cannot be avoided. But we have seen that *extreme* stress can have adverse effects at points throughout the reproductive process. It can lead to infertility, miscarriage, premature birth and perhaps even birth defects.

Why should this be? Darwinian minded researchers are increasingly of the opinion that the link between stress and "reproductive suppression" is an adaptation. We saw an example of this already when we noted that underweight women—women undergoing "nutritional stress"—become infertile. It turns out that there are a whole bunch of mechanisms that evolved to inhibit reproduction if living conditions for Hannah the hunter-gatherer were not promising. And if Hannah was under a lot of continuous stress, then conditions were probably not right for raising a baby. And so her body responded under the assumption that future conditions might be better for baby making.

- If she was not yet pregnant, her body suppressed her fertility.
- If she was recently pregnant, then her body triggered a miscarriage.
- If she was approaching full-term, then her body triggered a miscarriage; we call it a premature birth, but it's really just a late miscarriage.

What kinds of stress are known to have these troubling effects? And how much stress is too much? Surely going grocery shopping won't cause me to miscarry!?

Of course not. Going grocery shopping is a single, mildly stressful event that poses no risk by itself. At the worst, shopping just makes some of us a little irritable and tired.

In addition to severe weight loss, it turns out that one of the most powerful stressors is the loss of social support. So if you are unmarried, or your mate suddenly leaves you and you have no other friends or relatives in your life, then the evidence suggests that you have a somewhat increased risk for some form of reproductive suppression.

You can see why natural selection might have linked the loss of social support with reproductive suppression. A pregnant and soon-to-be breastfeeding woman and her baby would have had much better chances of surviving if mom had some help in procuring food and defending themselves from predators. Indeed, some anthropologists have argued that loss of social support would essentially have been a death sentence for a hunter-gatherer mother and baby.

For many of us, the levels of stress we encountered before pregnancy won't harm us or the baby during pregnancy. And the research is still clarifying the effects of stress on pregnancy, so don't let this knowledge add more stress to your pregnancy. No matter what, a major benefit of reducing stress is an increase in our quality of life: our mood improves, we are less likely to catch a cold, and…*we have the resources to parent well.*

THINKING AHEAD: YOUR PARENTING LIFESTYLE

Perhaps you think that now we are going to suggest an "everything-in-moderation" lifestyle. Exercise and reduce the stressors in your life and you'll be ready for parenthood, right? Well, we do believe that doing what you can to become a modern-day Hannah is a good idea for many women. Exercise, certainly. However, the problem of stress—before, during, and after pregnancy—is more complicated than that.

That's because the stress a person experiences is a function of two things: circumstances occurring in her life, and *how she perceives* those circumstances. The same intense lifestyle that one person finds exciting and gratifying can transform another into a complete basket case.

Take work. Jobs outside the home, in particular, are a common source of stress and frustration for many people. Others love what they do. Which are you? We've seen that Hannah's work life was very low-key. But of course, she never had the opportunity to choose a high-powered, fulfilling, lucrative career. Perhaps you do. If that's the case, then of course you needn't give it up. If it makes you feel energized and happy rather than comatose, then it's not going to be a health problem for you or your child. It will be a terrific thing.

More likely, though, you find yourself in a gray area here: you like the money your job pulls in, and you find some aspects of your work satisfying but other aspects irritating or stressful.

Whatever your situation, as a mom-to-be, you face a problem as old as womanhood: how to balance economic security with childcare. We know there are not many options for good, affordable childcare out there and this is a real problem that has yet to be addressed.

For the time being, consider this. When given the chance, women have always—and we mean "always" in the big sense of "throughout the history of the human species"—been interested in increasing their economic security and well-being. It is natural—universal, in fact—to seek status in our social group. Doing so has always been beneficial to offspring. Evolutionary theory does *not* lead to the conclusion that woman are mere baby-making machines designed to give birth to as many babies as possible and then devote themselves entirely to their care.

Parenting is hard work. So how do you establish a healthy lifestyle in preparation for the added stressor of a child in your life? How about this, for starters:

- Exercise more.
- Reduce or eliminate the things in your life that *you* find stressful, if you can.
- Keep doing the things that make you feel fulfilled and important to other people.
- Most importantly, strengthen your social support network and especially your relationship with your mate.

The last point is the most crucial of all. Now, while you have the time and energy, plan your family lifestyle together. Perhaps you can do this while driving to and from your childbirth class, which we will discuss in the next chapter.

Chapter 10

CHOOSING PRENATAL CARE

You live and live and listen to yourself. You watch as your body changes. One day you feel the baby moving, rising high inside you. Another day you feel it elsewhere. You live, feeling the baby as it does things.

-Nisa, a !Kung San hunter-gatherer woman

Prenatal care may include:

- prenatal monitoring,
- counseling, and
- preparation for labor and birth.

Our ancient friend Hannah the hunter-gatherer made it through without ultrasounds, nutritional counseling, or birth classes. So I suppose we could ask whether prenatal care is necessary at all.

That would be silly. The benefits of good prenatal care are unquestionable. The thing you really have to decide on is the kind of care you want. Could a brief peek from an evolutionary angle help you out?

As we'll see below, the person or practice you choose can have a big impact on how you feel throughout your pregnancy. Perhaps most important, in choosing your prenatal care provider you are heading down a path that will tend to influence where you give birth, your method of laboring, your approach to pain management during birth, who will attend the birth, and who will be taking care of you and your baby for a very, very short time postpartum.

RECENT DEVELOPMENTS

Who helps us give birth? Until the end of the 19th century, traditional midwives delivered American babies. But very quickly after that, the exclusively male and at times astoundingly sexist field of obstetrics began to compete for control of the birth process. Obstetricians initially dealt mostly with "abnormal deliveries," while midwives and general practitioners competed for "normal" births. Eventually, however, the well-organized physicians won out rather completely and took control of the vast majority of births in the U.S. Midwifery didn't disappear, but the traditional "home schooled" midwife virtually did. Beginning around 1930, only obstetrically trained and supervised midwives from recognized schools were allowed to practice.

The status of midwives has rebounded considerably as the natural childbirth movement attracted moms who were disillusioned with the way that doctors treated pregnancy and birth: as an illness rather than a normal process. The natural childbirth movement has been around since the 1930s, but it didn't really start catching on until the rise of the women's movement and the counterculture in the 1970s.

At the same time, however, new medical technologies like fetal monitors, newborn intensive care units (NICUs), ultrasounds, and drugs to induce or stop labor enhanced physicians' ability to medically assist in the birth process.

Many physicians are now powerful supporters of midwife care, and collaborate with them daily. Others clearly are not as supportive. Depending on the type of training they have and the laws passed by their state's legislature, midwives today may work under the supervision of physicians, in consultation with physicians, or independently.

Where we have our babies. In the U.S. at the beginning of the 20th century, virtually all infants were delivered at home. By 1940, about half of our babies were born in hospitals. By 1979, the transformation was complete: fully 99 percent of all American babies started life in a hospital.

Since then, the percentage of hospital births has dropped to a little over 90 percent. The other almost-10 percent of births in the U.S. today occur either in freestanding birthing centers or at home. Birthing centers—bed and breakfast-like places with suites that include kitchens, family rooms, bedrooms with queen-sized beds and, frequently, Jacuzzi tubs—account for 28 percent of these out-of-hospital births. Birthing centers are typically affiliated with a nearby hospital in the event of any emergency.

The other 72 percent of out-of-hospital births in the U.S. occur at home.

Healthy competition. Mainstream hospital practice into the 1970s demanded that infants be put in a nursery right after birth to prevent infection. Husbands were treated as sources of infection and pushed away from participation in the birth experience. In order to see his child being born, a Michigan man had handcuffed himself to his wife's hospital bed in defiance of the medical staff's insistence that he not be present.

Some couples responded by seeking out-of-hospital alternatives. The number of home births was slowly increasing, and birth centers were springing up all over the country. Hospitals responded to this challenge to their business by offering family-friendly birthing rooms on their premises and attempting to lighten up on the medical regimen i some ways.

This competition for pregnant moms has continued unabated up to the present day. The various providers out there are eager to attract you, the expectant customer.

YOUR MENU, MADAME

The upshot is that today, your prenatal/birthing choices are a confusing array of options and combinations, like an a la carte menu. On one extreme is the all-medical platter. If you order that, you will have an obstetrician and can give birth in a hospital, with feet up in stirrups in the lithotomy position, in a surgical-style delivery room. This is the selection a large number of women make, but often by default—many simply don't consider the alternatives.

At the other extreme is the home-style platter, a completely non-medical home birth with a midwife. Like many natural food dishes, it may not be as good for you as you might think.

The all-medical and home-style platters are, as we said, extremes. A healthy mom-to-be can opt for all sorts of interesting, eclectic combinations, choosing her own blend of midwifery and obstetrical medicine. As one of many possible examples, you could have a midwife-assisted hospital birth that includes pain medication or an epidural. Your prenatal care might in this case consist of a group of certified nurse midwives who work on a rotating basis in consultation with staff physicians.

Rather than try to elaborate on all the possible meals you could concoct, let's just clarify the basic menu a bit, keeping in mind that there are many permutations.

Choosing Where to Give Birth. Of course, the specific menu available to you is going to depend on the restaurant you choose. That is, deciding where you want to give birth will tend to influence how much medical intervention you'll have available to you during labor.

If you have a pre-existing medical condition that could require speedy medical assistance during labor, it goes without saying that you want to give birth in a hospital. The same goes if you have twins, or if your baby is in breech position.

Having a hospital birth today doesn't mean you have to be in a traditional sterile, surgical delivery room, though. In response to consumer pressure and competition from birthing centers, many hospitals have established "birthing rooms." These aren't quite like home, but they are fairly cozy and pleasant, and at any rate they are definitely an improvement over the old delivery room. At the same time, they provide you with immediate access to all the usual hospital technologies, except a cesarean section, which requires an operating room. (Since birthing rooms are in a hospital, the operating room is usually nearby, down the hall or on another floor.)

Usually you will know well ahead of time, during prenatal check-ups, if there is a complication that makes medical assistance during labor necessary. So for many women, a lower-tech birth center or home delivery is a real option.

If you fall into that category, then the best place for you to give birth is wherever you feel safest. Once you understand your options as well as some of the surprising truths about the evolution of human birth, you'll be in the best position to make an informed choice about what's best for you.

Finally, make some visits. Many places now invite expecting parents to visit or take classes that include tours of the facility. Why not take advantage of such opportunities? You have time!

Choosing Your Birth Attendant. To emphasize the connection between prenatal care choice and your birth experience, the table below is organized by types of birth attendants. For each category of birth attendant, it shows the type of training they have received, where you are most likely to have your birth, and the philosophy of care you might reasonably expect them to have.

Keep in mind that this is just a rough guide. Practitioners of each type vary in their attitudes and practices.

Darwinian common sense suggests that choosing the right person may be more important than choosing the right category of birth attendant. Evolutionary thinking reminds us that we are social creatures that evolved to coexist and depend on each other. We've seen in earlier chapters how a sense of social support, or the loss of it, can dramatically impact our health and our sense of well-being. That feeling of being cared for is also extremely beneficial when you are expecting. If you are lucky, you'll find that your prenatal care provider becomes another key person in your social support network.

COMPARISON OF DIFFERENT TYPES OF BIRTH ATTENDANTS

Type of Birth Attendant	Training	Typical Birth Setting	Typical Philosophy
Obstetrician	Medical school; 4 years residency in obstetrics and gynecology	Hospitals; birth centers	Surgeons, trained to deal with complicated deliveries; more likely than midwife to want to use medical intervention
Family physician	Medical school; 3 years residency in family practice, including at least 3 months in obstetrics and gynecology	Varies; more support home birth now than used to be the case	Varies widely; more likely than midwife to want to use medical intervention
Midwife: Certified Nurse Midwife (CNM)	Registered nurse with 2 years advanced practice in prenatal care and birth; certified by the American College of Nurse Midwives (ACNM)	Hospital or birth center, under the supervision of a physician; some attend home births	Midwifery is radically different from the medical approach; grew out of the tradition of woman helping each other give birth; emphasizes that pregnancy is a healthy and normal condition; openly dedicated to providing care that is sensitive to the mother's beliefs and concerns; tends to resist medical intervention unless absolutely necessary; advocates natural (drug-free) childbirth
Certified Professional Midwife (CPM)	Trained through an independent midwifery school or apprenticeship; certified by the North American Registry of Midwives (NARM); not required to have a college education	Birth centers or home; work in consultation with physicians rather than under their supervision	
Licensed Midwife (LM)	CNMs, CPMs, or independent midwives who meet state requirements for midwifery licensure; typically must pass a written and practical exam	Varies by practitioner and by state; roughly 25 percent of all states provide midwifery licensure	

PRENATAL MONITORING

At a minimum, prenatal monitoring means getting your vital signs checked regularly. Other noninvasive checks include counting and recording the number of fetal movements that occur within a given amount of time. For "natural parenting" advocates, though, controversy arises as soon as more invasive medical monitoring is considered. Why should the medical industry, with all its technological gizmos, intrude upon this normal biological process? After all, it is only in the past century that childbirth has been taken over by doctors.

The answer, of course, is that although women did without medical meddling for hundreds of thousands of years, they often died—and so did their babies. For humans, birth is actually a pretty dangerous process. Clearly, what's called for is some kind of balance between natural and medical approaches.

Also, given the information presented in previous chapters, you might understandably be concerned about your baby-to-be's health. It's scary, but we've seen that there are many ways that prenatal development can go wrong. Nature's universal child-making assembly line—your reproductive system—is far from invincible. As previous chapters have shown, many defects in baby-construction are detected early on by the body, resulting in miscarriage. But your body's "quality control" team is less than perfect. It is alarming to learn that of all infants born in North America, about 2-3 percent have major birth defects. Another 4-10 percent have "minor" defects that significantly reduce both the child and parents' quality of life.

So, you may very much want to know if your baby-to-be is developing normally. On the other hand, you may be wary of unnecessary medical intervention. As many of us are aware, doctors often feel they must protect themselves from lawsuits by using available medical technology. And who could blame them? That means that they will tend to recommend everything that will cover their legal behinds. Fortunately, many routine medical interventions during pregnancy are not dangerous. Unfortunately, if there are suspected issues, the more invasive medical technologies involve risks—small risks, but real ones. It's up to you to figure out which of the procedures recommended to you are really worth those risks.

Without getting into the tedious technical details that are readily available in other books and which, in any case, will keep changing as medical technology improves, the types of prenatal tests you may experience include:

- *In early pregnancy*—blood tests, glucose challenge test, ultrasounds, check for fetal heart beat
- *In later pregnancy*—fetal movement counts, a non-stress test, an oxytocin challenge test and, of course, an ultrasound.

If you have an increased risk of passing on a disorder, or if prenatal tests arouse concern, you may be asked to undergo more extensive testing. You may also be given the option to just monitor the situation, with more frequent ultrasound or a more sophisticated ultrasound. Invasive testing is usually something that happens when there is sustained concern.

The good news about prenatal testing in general is that it can put your mind at ease. When well-trained medical personnel administer these tests, and especially when more than one test is used, they are highly reliable—though not perfect—in detecting birth defects and other problems.

If you do need more invasive testing, there is some bad news. Some prenatal tests do pose a risk to your baby-to-be. For instance, 0.5-1.0 percent of fetuses that undergo amniocentesis miscarry because of the procedure. This risk of miscarriage is even a little higher for chorionic vitrus sampling, about 1.5-2.0 percent. However, to make matters even more complicated, these more invasive tests also tend to provide more accurate information than some of the others. Good health-care providers weigh these risks accordingly.

The ultrasound has become standard procedure for many OB/GYNs. Yet some natural parenting advocates steer women away from this test. This is an example of the kind of faulty thinking some of these people are prone to: Nature knows best, so if it's technology, then it's always bad. That simply isn't true! The plague was natural, too.

Ultrasound provides a lot of useful information, is noninvasive, and does not place the fetus at risk for miscarriage. Studies involving tens of thousands of infants and children exposed *in utero* to ultrasound have not detected any adverse effects. As with any medical procedure, check to ensure that a well-trained practitioner administers the test and that they are using the best available equipment. On the other hand, we recommend thinking twice before getting a super high contrast ultrasound, just to see baby-to-be in HD. There is some evidence to suggest that the "sounds" in the ultrasound are unpleasant for the baby—routine ultrasounds are just fine.

In our humble opinion, letting nature take its course and choosing not to do any prenatal screening might mean having a baby with serious health problems or birth defects that would be best treated at birth. We are lucky to live in an age where we can, if we desire, choose to get some help from highly sophisticated medical know-how.

Weighing the costs and benefits of a procedure can be difficult and a little nerve-racking, though. You can expect to get a lot of input from various sources with conflicting but firmly held opinions. Asking yourself and your prenatal care provider these questions can help:

- What is the risk that your baby will have birth defects?
- How risky is the procedure that you are considering?
- How hard will it be to conceive again if you have a miscarriage?
- How do you feel about having a baby with birth defects?
- How do you feel about aborting a baby with known birth defects?

Evolutionary theory is useful because it reminds us of how vulnerable our babies-to-be really are. But it cannot make highly personal, moral decisions for you. Only you can do that.

For reasons that make evolutionary sense, making decisions about prenatal testing—or any aspect of pregnancy and birth—is much easier if your care provider gives you the time of day. Midwives are explicitly dedicated to doing just that, but of course they don't have a monopoly on sensitive care. Many medically oriented providers specialize in prenatal care and delivery because they find it satisfying to help women bring a new life into this world. The stereotype of a cold, uncaring physician with no interpersonal skills is just that—a stereotype. The stereotype of a midwife as a new age granola-eating aging hippy hell bent on indoctrinating you into earth motherhood and the total rejection of all technology is just as misleading.

So, you are going to want to interview prospective prenatal care providers and choose someone you're comfortable with.

COUNSELING

Prenatal care does not have to mean medical care. That's really up to you. But, unless you've had extensive training in pregnancy and childbirth, the sense of security and support that you get from having a well-informed, caring individual helping you make decisions about exercise, diet, and stress-control is enormously beneficial.

In the U.S., the absence of prenatal care for low-income moms-to-be is a serious public health issue. High quality prenatal care beginning early in pregnancy is consistently related to birth weight and infant survival. Yet according to the Children's Defense Fund, 18 percent of pregnant women in the U.S. wait until after the first trimester to seek prenatal care, and 4 percent delay until the end of pregnancy or never get any at all! These women often lead very stressful lives and would benefit greatly from early supportive care.

So if you can afford good prenatal care, take advantage of it and consider yourself fortunate. Try to find someone with experience that you both respect and like as a person. You want someone warm and caring enough to take your questions and concerns seriously. They should be willing to provide a reasonable amount of emotional support as you adjust to parenthood. If your provider seems preoccupied, avoids responding to your concerns, or is unwilling to deviate from standard procedure but won't explain why, dump her/him. You deserve better.

PREPARATION FOR LABOR AND BIRTH

How many sitcom episodes have lampooned hilarious birth education classes? How many excruciatingly painful looking deliveries have you seen depicted in the media? Guess what? They *are* hilarious, and it *is* painful.

Go ahead, take a childbirth class. Hannah the hunter-gatherer never had them, but she probably got some information and help from women in her social group. These classes can be fun, and they provide a structured time for you and your mate to think about what's ahead, to ask questions, and to share your experiences with other parents-to-be. Note that we emphasize that you *and your mate* should go together to these classes. Going to birth class is an easy and enjoyable way for your partner to provide emotional support to the person who is going to be doing the hard work of labor soon: you. Drag them there, if necessary.

Often birth classes and prenatal care are linked. So you'll want to find out about the classes at the same time that you are interviewing your prospective care provider about the questions raised above. While some will advocate a specific approach—Lamaze, Bradley, or "Birthing Within," to name a few— most are eclectic. In addition to providing parents-to-be with a preview of labor and delivery, including some simple anatomy and physiology, a main goal is almost always to teach techniques for relaxation and breathing that can help you stay focused and relaxed (ha!) during contractions.

EPILOGUE (DR. CRATON)

So far we've made a few passing remarks suggesting that giving birth is er…challenging (see "ha" above). But we haven't made a big deal out of it. The time has come for that to change. I say this with enormous regret. No amount of childbirth education could have prepared me for my wife's first labor. I have literally spent years trying to understand what really happened. After all this time—my firstborn is now 26 years old—I have come to know the ultimate truth about childbirth. Not just my daughter's birth, or my son's birth, but *birth as it has been designed by natural selection*. It's the ultimate truth, which you would think would be something that you would want to know about. But you're not going to like it.

In fact, if you are expecting, I beg you not to buy the sequel that we are currently writing. It begins with a chapter that explains why human birth is so challenging. In fact, if you ever plan to be expecting at any time in your life, I think you better skip the next book.

Ok, ok. You can buy the next book when it comes out. It will have many useful chapters on childrearing from a Darwinian perspective that you may enjoy. Check our website (darwinschild.com) for more information.

But really, I mean it. When the next book on Darwin's child comes out, don't read the chapter on birth.

Happy parenting.

INDEX

Y